24 LETTERS
from NEW YORK

24 LETTERS
from NEW YORK

RISE TO YOUR FULL POTENTIAL
ONE ARCHETYPE AT A TIME

MRIANNA

ISBN: 979-8-9928243-0-8

for
MY GIACOMO–MY ANCHOR & MY HORIZON;
MY PARENTS–THE PILLARS OF MY BEING;
MY UNCLE–THE ANGEL OF OUR HEARTS.

CONTENTS

PROLOGUE

THE 24 LETTERS

There is a certain magic to letters.

They are a testament to presence,
an artful pause in a world that rushes forward.

Personal. Timeless. Intimate.

They are crafted with care,
unfolding not in haste,
but through contemplation,
allowing meaning to
settle,
expand,
and resonate.

This book is a collection of such letters.

24 invitations to
challenge,
awaken,
and align yourself
with the extraordinary within.

They are invitations
to remember what you have always known,
but have been too busy to notice.
Invitations to pause,
to question,
to dream.

They are meant to be
returned,
revisited,
rediscovered—
each time offering a different insight
because you, too, will be different.

August 27th, 2021.
The day my journey began in New York—
a metropolis where ambition and solitude
share the same crowded streets,
where dreams are born
in the same moment
others are surrendered.

It is there that 24 archetypes revealed themselves—
emerging through strangers and silence,
through conversation and stillness,
in the unnoticed spaces
where human nature gently stirs.

They rose in moments of doubt,
in seasons of undoing and becoming,
in the quiet hours
when clarity returned
like an old and patient friend.

Each letter carries
the voice of a distinct archetype,
guiding you toward
what Aristotle called *eudaimonia*:
not the fleeting happiness of modern life,
but a deep flourishing
where virtue, wisdom,
and purposeful action converge.

It is the art of becoming fully yourself,
living true to your essence,
embracing who you were always meant to be,
before the world told you who you should be.

Some letters will feel
like tender validation,
others,
like an insistent spark,
drawing you toward
the fullness of your potential.

Together,
they form 24 archetypes for
the profound journey of
becoming with purpose.

This book is not about reaching a final destination.
It is about the extraordinary journey itself—
the emerging,
the evolving,
the stretching toward something greater
with intention and courage.

It is about rising after failure,
trusting yourself and the path ahead,
surrendering what no longer serves you,
and daring to create the future
instead of inheriting it.

Before you turn the page,
acknowledge exactly where you are.

Not where you should be.
Not where you once were.
But precisely here,
in this moment.

Then step forward—
for your becoming depends on it.

Welcome to the 24 LETTERS *from* NEW YORK.
They are yours now.

PART I:

THE FOUNDATIONS *of* EMPOWERMENT

Letter 1: Dear Visionary
THE CALL TO RISE

To rise is to trust that your restless dreams are not burdens, but invitations—the future calling you beyond comfort into your becoming.

There comes a moment
when the world you have known
no longer feels like enough.

A quiet unease stirs within you—
a knowing that there is more.
Not from ingratitude,
but from unrealized potential.

Something within you knows
there is more—
to see,
to become,
to create.

This knowing is your call to rise,
a call so magnetic and unfaltering,
it refuses to be ignored.

Throughout history,
those who have shaped our world
have felt this same stirring,
this same tension between
what is and what could be.

Plato, in the *Allegory of the Cave*,
spoke of those who turn toward the light,
daring to see what others cannot.

Yet to see more is to be burdened by more—
to know unsettling truths,
to envision futures that
do not yet exist.

This is the visionary's challenge:
walking between worlds,
holding both the reality that is
and the one that could be.

Such awareness demands a strength
few will ever understand
and even fewer will recognize.

T.S. Eliot once wrote,
"only those who will risk going too far can possibly find
out how far one can go."

This risk is not recklessness
but an act of faith,
trusting that even in faltering,
the very attempt will reshape you.

The visionary does not conform to
the world as it is
but dares to imagine
what has yet to be seen.

But why does the pursuit of a vision feel
so heavy at times?

Your mind naturally recoils
from the unknown.
The greater the vision,
the stronger the resistance
you will encounter.

This is not a flaw.
It is your brain's way of
tethering you to
safety and familiarity.

Your doubts are not
evidence of inadequacy,
they are proof of your becoming,
of reaching beyond
what once felt safe and known.

The voice asking,
"Who am I to do this?"
competes with another asking,
"Who am I not to?"

"The impediment to action advances action.
What stands in the way becomes the way,"
wrote Marcus Aurelius.

Every obstacle between you and your vision
is not there to stop you.
It exists to refine you.

When you feel alone in your vision, remember:
You are not lost.
You are ahead.

Margaret Mead wrote that
significant change always begins with
"a small group of thoughtful,
committed citizens."

Everett Rogers captured this truth in
his *diffusion curve*:
where innovation begins quietly,
with the few,
before echoing widely
through the many,
until what was once unthinkable
becomes the new norm.

History, it seems,
rarely embraces visionaries
in their own time.

Socrates was condemned for questioning too deeply.
Galileo was silenced for seeing too far.
Joan of Arc was dismissed as mad until
she altered the fate of a nation.

Those who disrupt established patterns and
challenge the comfort of convention,
are often met with resistance,
or even ridicule.

Yet it is precisely this disruption that forges the future.

Every structure we live within—
our institutions,
our philosophies,
our technologies—
was once a radical idea
in the mind of someone
who dared to think differently.

The probability of success is never certain,
but movement creates possibilities that
stillness never will.

David Bohm spoke of *active information*:
the notion that consciousness itself
may create the very potentialities of the universe.
Consciousness is not a passive observer of reality,
but an active participant in its unfolding.

Martin Heidegger's concept of *being*
also reminds us:
We do not simply exist,
we actively engage with the world,
shaping it and being shaped,
through our intentions,
choices,
and actions.

Every moment invites us to meet the world
not with resignation,
but with response.

Align yourself with the frequency of creation,
of reinvention,
of innovation,
wholly and without hesitation.

For the thoughts that keep you restless,
the dreams that burn in your chest,
the ideas that refuse to let you settle,
they are not distractions.
They are redirections—
calls toward a vision
longing to be embodied.

They speak to what Deci and Ryan
defined as *intrinsic motivation*:
the internal resonance
with your purpose.

To rise is not to wait for certainty.
It is to summon the courage
to affirm possibility amid uncertainty,
to recognize that holding on to the familiar
can unravel your becoming.

You do not need to see the entire path.
You only need to take the first step,
trusting that clarity
will meet you in motion,
not in waiting.

Rise.

Not because it is easy.
Not because the world will applaud.
But because the voice within you
demands to be heard—
it was never meant to be silenced.

Letter 2: Dear Sovereign Mind

MASTERING THOUGHT, SHAPING REALITY

> *Our thoughts, often formed in silence, build the*
> *foundation of our perception, shaping not just*
> *how we see the world, but how we live within it.*

There is a force within you
more potent than circumstance,
more defining than fate.

It is not talent or ambition.
It is what governs them all:
your mind.

Your thoughts do not merely reflect reality,
they construct it.

This is not an illusion of self-help rhetoric,
but an undeniable philosophical and
neurological truth.

The way you think determines
what you perceive,
what you pursue, and,
ultimately,
who you become.

Left untended,
the mind resembles a battleground of
reactions,
inherited beliefs,
and unconscious fears.

Descartes once declared *"cogito, ergo sum"*—
"I think, therefore I am."
He positioned thought as the foundation
not just of existence,
but of our entire experienced reality.

Plato, too, understood this:
his concept of *nous* sought truth
beyond appearances—
a higher order beyond the visible.

The sovereign mind, then,
is one that does not accept
the given world at face value.

It reaches
for clarity,
for coherence,
for what lies beyond.

And Kant's *transcendental idealism* affirms this:
we do not experience the world as it is,
but as it appears to us,
filtered through
our senses,
cognition,
and prior understanding.

Our mind refracts the world in ways unique to
our experiences,
biases,
and expectations.

This represents both a limitation and a power.

For while objective truth
may remain elusive,
we can refine perception,
hone our awareness,
and expand our understanding.

Aaron Beck reinforced this:
our belief systems and automatic thoughts
are the unseen architects of our perception.

These thought patterns,
often formed in the shadows of consciousness,
lay the foundation for
how we experience
every moment of our lives.

Carl Jung deepens this idea with
his notion of the *collective unconscious*:
a shared pool of human experience,
archetypes,
and symbols,
stretching beyond personal awareness,
subtly guiding us in ways we rarely perceive.

The narratives we carry,
about who we are and how the world works,
govern not only our behaviors,
but the very reality we inhabit.

There is no neutral perception of the world,
only interpretation through the architecture of thought.

Donald Hoffman takes this further:
our perception did not evolve for accuracy,
but for utility—
offering a functional interface,
not a faithful reflection of reality.

We do not see the world as it is.
We see our model of it.

The mind constructs an interface,
discovering what it expects to find,
whether limitation or possibility.

Yet Daniel Kahneman
identified *"system 2 thinking"*:
the slower,
more deliberate mode of reflection that
allows us to question assumptions and
transcend biases.

In the absence of this reflective awareness,
our minds default to reactivity.
For the brain rewires itself
around the thoughts
we revisit most.

When those thoughts go unchecked,
the mind becomes
a cacophony of fears,
conditioned responses,
and borrowed beliefs
masquerading as truth.

Our deepest convictions curate our experiences.
They shape not only how we see the world,
but what we are willing to believe is possible
within it.

This is why self-fulfilling prophecies
are not mystical concepts,
but cognitive inevitabilities.

Albert Bandura called this *self-efficacy*:
when we believe in our ability to succeed,
we are more likely to take actions that
align with that belief.

Our thoughts crystallize into beliefs.
Our beliefs manifest as actions.
Our actions define our lived experience.

Nietzsche warned:
"The individual has always had to struggle
to keep from being overwhelmed by the tribe.
If you try it,
you will be lonely often,
and sometimes frightened.
But no price is too high to pay
for the privilege of owning yourself."

To own your mind is to stand in your truth,
to reclaim the power to live
with intention,
not imitation.

This is freedom not only from
the narratives imposed by others,
but from the pull of belonging,
the lure of validation.

The question is not
whether your mind shapes reality,
but whether you consciously
direct your thoughts,
or merely dwell within them.

Just as thought defines the individual,
it also defines civilizations.

The Renaissance did not begin with discovery,
but with a rebellion of thought
against medieval dogma.

The Enlightenment was not an age of invention,
but a revolution in cognitive autonomy.

History's most profound transformations
did not begin with weapons or wealth,
but with ideas powerful enough
to rewrite the human story.

A nation is only as strong as the minds that compose it.
A culture is only as wise as the thoughts it nurtures.
A person is only as free as their ability to think
for themselves.

The mind's greatest adversary is not external chaos,
but internal rigidity—
the unwillingness to entertain
uncertainty without fear.

Nassim Taleb's idea of *antifragility* reminds us:
complex systems (and minds) grow stronger
not despite stress,
but because of it.

The sovereign mind does not break under pressure,
it extracts wisdom from disruption.

John Dewey challenged
a central assumption in Western thought:
that knowledge precedes experience,
rather than arising from it.

But it is action that transforms perception,
for knowing is not what enables us to act.
It is what emerges because we do.

Heisenberg's *uncertainty principle*
offers a fitting metaphor:
perfect knowledge remains impossible.
The very act of observation alters
what is observed.

And yet
we yearn for immutable truths and
definitive answers.
But reality resists such simplification.

The mind that demands absolute knowledge
becomes a prisoner of its own limitations,
mistaking momentary understanding
for ultimate truth.

The sovereign mind
does not retreat into false certainty,
it learns to move with uncertainty,
not against it,
seeing in ambiguity
a field of possibility.

It does not seek to eliminate it,
it meets it
with steadiness,
with humility,
with grace.

And so,
if the mind is the lens through which
meaning takes form,
nurture it with reverence.

If your thoughts are
the architects of your experience,
guard them vigilantly.

If your mind determines your becoming,
shape it—
with wisdom,
with clarity,
with compassion,
with unwavering intent.

For in mastering your mind,
you become the deliberate composer
of your life.

Letter 3: Dear Alchemist

TRANSFORMING STRUGGLE INTO STRENGTH

> *Pain is not your punishment but your crucible—*
> *transforming what would break you into the gold*
> *of who you are meant to become.*

There will be moments when life tests you,
not gently,
but with fire—
with weight,
with trials,
with breaking points that
threaten to unmake you.

They arrive unbidden,
indifferent to fairness,
unmoved by your readiness.

They do not ask if you are strong enough.
Prepared enough.
Willing enough.

They come only to see what you will become.

Pain is universal.
To transmute suffering into wisdom,
into strength,
into something unshakable,
this is the mark of the alchemist.

Nietzsche called it *amor fati*—
the love of fate:
"I wish to learn, ever more deeply,
to perceive the necessity
in all things as beauty;
for in doing so,
I become one who renders the world beautiful."

The alchemists do not curse the fire.
They step into it willingly,
knowing it will burn away the inessential,
leaving only what is strong enough to last.

Seneca taught that obstacles are not hindrances,
but teachers.
"Difficulties strengthen the mind", he wrote,
"just as labor does the body."

The weight that presses upon you
is not blocking your path,
it is forging your resilience.

The greater the trial,
the greater the opportunity of transformation.

To become whole,
to evolve into something greater,
you must not only ascend toward light
but descend into depth.

Hermann Hesse
often wrote of transformation
as an *alchemical process*—
a journey of dissolution, purification, and rebirth.

Alchemy, at its core,
is the art of transmutation,
turning base metal into gold,
the ordinary into the extraordinary.

What you endure is not meant to break you.
It is meant to forge you.

Adversity rewires the mind to
collapse under pressure
or emerge stronger than before.

This is known as *post-traumatic growth*:
the phenomenon where those who endure
emerge not merely intact,
but profoundly changed.

They develop greater clarity, resilience, and purpose
not in spite of their struggles,
but because of them.

Yet growth through adversity
does not unfold by default.
It must be chosen,
nurtured,
and embodied.

Some remain trapped in suffering,
reliving the same pain,
the same loss,
the same fear.

The difference lies in perception.

It is what Viktor Frankl called the *last human freedom*:
the ability to choose one's response,
to assign meaning to suffering,
and through that meaning,
to transcend it.

Your mind will follow the meaning you give it.

If you see adversity as destruction,
it will destroy you.
If you see it as transformation,
it will remake you.

Cognitive reframing teaches us that
our interpretation of events
determines our response.

The alchemist does not ask,
"Why did this happen to me?"
but rather,
"What can I create from this?"

History belongs to those who
choose to transform adversity.

Nelson Mandela spent 27 years in prison.
It did not diminish him,
it refined his purpose.

Helen Keller,
born into silence and darkness,
did not curse her fate,
she illuminated the world.

Dante Alighieri,
exiled from his homeland,
wrote *the Divine Comedy*
not as a lament,
but as an odyssey through suffering
toward transcendence.

The greatest art,
the most profound philosophies,
the breakthroughs that altered human history,
often began as suffering alchemized into creation.

And societies, too, are defined by struggle.

Civilizations that resist change decay.
Those that embrace it thrive.

What is true for societies is true for you.

The Japanese art of *kintsugi* teaches us:
brokenness is not
meant to be hidden,
but honored.
Cracks are filled with gold,
turning fractures into art.

Our scars are not signs of ruin but of resilience.

We are not meant to erase our scars,
nor to conceal the moments that
transformed us.

Every fracture tells a story,
every imperfection carries wisdom.

True strength is not in appearing unbroken.
It is in embracing our wholeness,
knowing that healing
does not erase the past,
but elevates it
into something greater.

Whatever you are facing now, remember:
It is not here to defeat you.
It is not here to reduce you.
It is here to awaken you.

Stand in its presence.

Let it strip away the inessential.
Let it refine you, not ruin you.
Let it make you gold.

Letter 4: Dear Warrior of Will

THE ART OF DISCIPLINE

Greatness is not born from privilege, talent, or luck —
it is forged in the quiet battle of will.

You wage a battle every day.
Not in grand arenas,
but in silence,
in moments
when no one is watching.

It is the battle between
discipline and distraction,
action and hesitation,
the self that seeks growth
and the self that seeks comfort.

To master yourself is to master this battle,
and mastery begins with will.

The world tells you that greatness is about
talent,
luck,
or privilege.

But history tells a different story.

It belongs to those who command themselves.
Those who refuse to be ruled by impulse,
who choose:
discipline over indulgence,
perseverance over ease.

To will something
is not simply to wish for it,
but to commit fully,
aligning thought and action to
bring it into being.

William James argued that
belief is not a passive state,
but an *act of will.*

His *Will to Believe* is not about blind faith.
It is about the courage to commit
before certainty arrives,
to act despite incomplete evidence,
to forge conviction through effort.

Diogenes the Cynic, and later the Stoics,
especially Epictetus,
knew that self-sufficiency (*autarkeia*)
is the true form of freedom and excellence.

In the words of Epictetus:
Though we cannot control external events,
our perceptions and judgments
remain entirely within our power.

The Stoics called it *apatheia*:
freedom from disturbing passions
through rational self-discipline.

Aristotle identified it as
the triumph over *akrasia*:
weakness of will.
He understood that
living virtuously required
not just knowledge of what is right,
but the discipline to act accordingly.

You are not meant to be tamed,
but to be redirected
with purpose,
not permission.

Schopenhauer,
in *the World as Will and Representation*,
saw existence as driven by an unstoppable will,
a blind force that compels all life to act.

Yet humans alone possess something more:
conscious will—
the ability to direct action through
deliberate intent.

Belief is not a passive acknowledgement of what is,
but the current that carries what becomes.

Those who wait for certainty remain stagnant.
Those who choose belief,
and the will to move forward
despite uncertainty,
are the ones
who alter the course of their lives.

For decades, psychologists have asked:
why do some rise,
while others remain unchanged?

It is not intelligence,
nor motivation.
It is willpower.

The battle between impulse and discipline,
between comfort and mastery,
is waged in the mind.

The prefrontal cortex must quiet
the primitive pull of the limbic system.

To govern oneself
is to direct the mind
toward long-term vision,
rather than fleeting pleasure.

Every time you honor
a commitment to yourself,
every time you rise
when it would be easier to rest,
you reinforce your
inner framework of resilience.

And the more you fortify that foundation,
the less fragile you become.

The *marshmallow experiment*,
a landmark psychological study on self-control,
found that children who delayed gratification
outperformed their peers in nearly
every measure of success decades later.

The world bends to those
who can command themselves.

Stanford psychologist Kelly McGonigal
defines *willpower* as:
the ability to do what matters most,
even when it is difficult—
choosing long-term values over short-term urges.

The warrior of will does not allow
temporary pleasure to sabotage
permanent greatness.

The ones who built empires,
wrote the philosophies,
composed the masterpieces,
they did not wait for permission.

Leonardo da Vinci filled thousands of pages
with sketches, ideas, and studies,
not because anyone told him to,
but because his will demanded it.

Miyamoto Musashi, the legendary samurai,
relentlessly honed his swordsmanship,
not out of obligation,
but because he believed that
mastery over one's craft
wasn't merely the pursuit of skill,
but a gateway to mastering life itself.

Marie Curie defied societal constraints
to become the first woman
to win the Nobel prize twice,
refusing to let external limitations
dictate her potential.

In every society,
in every era,
the division is not between
the privileged and the underprivileged,
nor between the lucky and the unlucky.

The true division is between
those who command themselves
vs. those who are ruled by impulse;
those who act despite difficulty
vs. those who wait for the perfect moment
that never arrives;
those who create their lives
vs. those who react to life.

No one controls the timing of opportunity,
the randomness of hardship,
the chaos of external events.

But what remains constant,
the one variable that
tilts probability in your favor,
is your will.

Game theory teaches:
those who prepare consistently,
even in the absence of immediate reward,
are those best positioned
when opportunity arrives.

The disciplined mind stacks the odds.
It prepares,
it persists,
it adapts.

It is not at the mercy of circumstances.
It creates conditions where success becomes
more likely,
more frequent,
more inevitable.

The world is unpredictable.
Your will is the only certainty you own.

If you wish to create, command yourself.
If you wish to lead, command yourself.
If you wish to rise beyond what you were given,
command yourself.

Your will is your weapon.
Your discipline is your foundation.
And in mastering both,
you design the arc of your becoming.

Do not wait for permission.
Do not wait for the right moment,
the right conditions.

Discipline is your steadfast ally.
Will,
your unyielding force.

Stand rooted in their confluence,
for it is there that
inner sovereignty is born—
a silent dominion
where thought refines will,
and will ignites purpose.

Letter 5: Dear Keeper of Energy

THE POWER OF DIRECTED INTENTION

What you give your energy to becomes your life.
A scattered mind depletes; a focused mind creates.

The most valuable currency you possess
is not time, talent,
or even knowledge.

It is energy—
the source of your existence,
the pulse behind every act of creation,
the invisible thread pulling you forward.

To be the keeper of your energy demands awareness.
Discernment.
The courage to say no.
The wisdom to know what is worthy of your life force.

Quantum physicists speak of
quantum potentiality:
energy existing in multiple states
until collapsed through
observation.

As William James observed,
your *selective interest* determines
what materializes in your life.

For what you give your energy to,
you give your life to.
And if you do not claim it,
the world will.

Spinoza spoke of *Oneness*—
not as an abstract idea,
but as the profound truth that
your energy is inseparable from
the universe itself.

It moves through you,
sculpts you,
ripples into everything.

When you align with this truth,
you stop fighting against
the flow of life and
start moving with it.

You become part of a greater whole,
effortlessly shaping your own path
while contributing to the greater flow of existence.

Teilhard de Chardin called this
the *Divine Milieu*:
an animating presence
guiding existence toward
complexity, evolution, and higher being.

And Bergson's *élan vital*,
the raw, creative impulse of life,
reminds us that energy is not just for vitality.
It is for transformation,
for expansion,
for becoming.

To wield your energy is not to contain it,
but to direct it—
deliberately,
artfully,
fearlessly.

Resist it, and you lose your way.
Move with it, and you find ease.
Align with it, and you move in harmony with all that is.

Eastern philosophy teaches that
the *Tao* is a current,
flowing effortlessly.

True strength is not in control,
but in surrendering to the flow
while steering with intention.

Csikszentmihalyi's *flow* reveals that
peak performance is not a product of
stress or sheer effort,
but of deep alignment
where challenge meets skill,
and self-consciousness
dissolves into pure engagement.

It is the moment
when action and awareness merge,
when thought gives way to presence,
when energy no longer scatters,
but gathers,
and begins to build.

In this state,
time bends,
distractions fade,
and every movement feels
both effortless and divine.

Flow is not forced.
It is entered.

Not through pushing harder,
but through tuning in—
by being fully absorbed
in the moment,
yet continuously expanding.

As Carl Rogers said,
"The good life is a process,
not a state of being.
It is a direction,
not a destination."

Your energy is what moves you in that direction.
Not distractions.
Not empty ambition.
Not busyness disguised as progress.

The brain is an energy-intensive machine.
Yet modern life keeps it
overstimulated, fractured, exhausted.

Decision fatigue,
information overload,
the invisible weight of competing priorities—
these are not signs of productivity,
they are symptoms of depletion.

The greatest minds didn't just seek knowledge,
they protected their focus.
Not because they lacked capacity,
but because they understood a deeper truth:
Scattered energy vanishes into nothingness.
Directed energy tunes the world to their frequency.

Yet our world moves
with an urgency we didn't choose,
not with the intention
we were born to create from.

Advertising does not sell products,
it hijacks attention.

Social structures do not cultivate focus,
they thrive on distraction.

Industries profit off your exhaustion.

Those who do not fiercely guard their energy
become vessels for someone else's agenda—
they build the dreams of others
while their own wither.

Resisting these clamors requires
what Michel Foucault
called *counter-conduct*:
a deliberate rebellion against
the subtle systems of control.

Societies that understand energy flourish.
Those that squander it collapse.

And if this is true for civilizations,
it is true for you.

Those who scatter their energy
become fragile, exhausted, and lost.
Those who harness it become unshakable,
thriving through disruption.
For your energy directs the course of your life.

You do not need more time.
You do not need more motivation.
You do not need more resources.

Do not pour your energy into what drains you.
Reclaim it for what propels you forward.

And so,
ask yourself:
Where is your energy flowing?
What are you unconsciously giving your life force to?
What distractions are stealing your purpose's fuel?

Your energy is finite,
but when guided by intention,
it becomes infinite in impact.

Use it to create.
To elevate.
To build.

Your energy is your imprint.

Honor it with kindness.
Protect it with compassion.
Align it with purpose.

PART II:

THE PSYCHOLOGY *of* TRANSFORMATION

Letter 6: Dear Stillness Seeker

ACHIEVING STILLNESS IN MOTION

Stillness is not the absence of movement; it is the presence of consciousness within every movement.

In a culture that glorifies speed,
stillness is an act of rebellion—
a refusal to equate
busyness with value,
constant motion with progress,
and exhaustion with success.

Stillness is not stagnation.
It is not withdrawal.
It is power contained.
It is where thought is honed,
where intuition deepens,
where action is no longer impulsive,
but intentional.

To live in Csikszentmihalyi's *flow*
is to embody both
stillness and motion,
presence and purpose,
awareness and action.

Stillness is not a cessation of energy,
it is its most harmonious form:
a cadence that dances with the rhythm of life,
balancing effort with ease.

It is not inaction,
but a refinement of movement.
It is not aimless motion,
but purposeful momentum—
what the ancient Chinese called
effortless action *(wu wei)*.

To practice stillness in motion is to
stay grounded in the now
while mindfully moving toward
what has yet to become.
It is action from centered presence,
not fragmented reactivity.

Heidegger, in *Being and Time*, reminds us:
"Temporality temporalizes as a future
which makes present in the process of having been."

The past does not just vanish,
the future does not just come to pass,
the now is not a static point,
they interweave.

Edmund Husserl's notion of
lived experience (*Erlebnis*)
challenges the idea of time
as a series of discrete points.

For Husserl, time is a living structure,
where past, present, and future
converge within consciousness.
Each moment is infused with
echoes of the past and
anticipations of the future.

To be still is to stand fully in its center.

Yet we hold on to a past that no longer exists,
chase a future we hesitate to pursue,
and evade the present through
distraction or doubt.

To live in stillness is
to live beyond the anxiety of
what's to come and the weight of
what has come before—
to fully inhabit
the richness of the now.

Hans-Georg Gadamer stressed *historicity*:
the idea that our future
cannot be separate from
our present and past.

Our thoughts are not born in a vacuum,
they are reflections of the traditions, ideas,
and experiences that precede us.

To commemorate history is not
to become mired in it,
but to learn from it,
to recognize its patterns,
explore its possibilities,
and carve a wiser future.

Kierkegaard once said:
"Life can only be understood backwards,
but it must be lived forwards."

In this paradox of existence,
we seek meaning in hindsight as
we forge ahead in uncertainty.

We make choices blind to their full significance,
for we only comprehend their wisdom
in retrospect.

The heart of living is found in this tension:
to learn with openness,
to move forward with uncertainty,
and to trust that clarity will follow.

Stillness grants us that inward gaze,
a reflective space where
awareness deepens and
meaning quietly takes shape.

It is within these rare moments of silence that
the mind renews itself,
untangles complexity,
and reaches the edges of profound insight.

Society conditions us to fear silence,
mistaking it for emptiness.

Yet silence,
in reality,
is the wellspring of clarity.

The artist finds inspiration in solitude.
The philosopher attains wisdom in contemplation.
The strategist sits in silence and builds vision.

Every great movement,
every epistemological revolution,
every spiritual awakening
was birthed in stillness.

The world celebrates only constant motion,
forgetting that without stillness,
there would be no clarity
from which action could follow.

The erosion of stillness
is the erosion of inner orientation and reflection.

 As Simone Weil said:
"Attention is the rarest and purest form of generosity."

To engage in stillness is to reclaim attention,
to direct it not toward
what is allegedly urgent,
but toward what is essential.

The Japanese idea of *zanshin*,
the state of relaxed alertness,
captures this duality—
the capacity to be fully present,
yet poised to move boldly
into the next moment.

It is this presence that crystallizes purpose,
and this readiness that carries your vision
beyond mere intention —
into form, into time, into being.

For when mind and movement are aligned,
the future begins to articulate itself
in the language of the now.

Such harmony echoes the wisdom of *Taoism*,
where Lao Tzu wrote: "Those who flow as life flows
know they need no other force."

This is where effort and ease coalesce,
where time feels suspended,
where you are fully absorbed in the present moment,
yet slowly advancing toward your greatest self.

When the world demands urgency, pause.
When your mind is crowded with noise,
silence it with intention.

Let the quiet places teach you
what the world forgot to say.
For in stillness, clarity is found.
And in that reclamation,
you return to the center of your truth.

Letter 7: Dear Growth Seeker

A QUIET QUEST

True growth is not about acquiring more information or accolades; it is about the quiet, ongoing evolution—a journey of unfolding, questioning, and becoming.

Growth is not an achievement.
It is a quiet quest.
It is not an end point.
It is an ongoing process of change and alignment.

It does not declare itself in grand moments,
but in the subtle,
in the barely perceptible shifts of thought,
in the silent choices that
carry the greatest weight.

Growth is not loud.
It does not bellow for validation,
nor rise for applause.

It stands without confirmation.
It is a testimony unto itself.
It is steady.
Persistent.
Insistent.

You were not meant to stagnate,
nor were you meant to rush toward an end.

You are a process, not a product.
A symphony, not a single note.

The question is not, *"Who am I?"*,
but rather,
"Who am I becoming?"

All of existence moves.
The cosmos expands.
The seasons shift.
The tides rise and fall.

To resist growth is to deny
the very rhythm life moves to.

Plotinus spoke of *the One*,
from which all things originate:
a singular, infinite, and transcendent source,
perfect, formless, and beyond comprehension.

From *the One* emanates a cascading hierarchy of being:
first *Nous* (Divine Intellect),
then *Psyche* (World Soul),
and finally, the material world.

Each emanation moves further from its source,
becoming more fragmented and
conditioned by multiplicity.

Yet all that flows from *the One*
carries within it an intrinsic longing to return,
not a physical movement,
but an inward spiritual ascent.

This ascent is not about striving outward,
but about dissolving the illusion of separation
and remembering the unity that has always been.

For the highest realization of the self
is not found in accumulation or achievement,
but in the quiet return to what you already are.

You are not born complete.
You are not meant to remain static.
You are in a perpetual state of unfolding.

To seek growth is not to seek perfection.
It is to recognize that
your nature is one of expansion,
not toward a final form,
but toward an ever-evolving complexity.

Jean Piaget speaks to this unfolding:
"Every acquisition of accommodation
becomes material for assimilation,
but assimilation always resists new accommodations."

We do not merely absorb new knowledge.
We reforge our very way of thinking to accommodate it.

Pirsig, in his *Metaphysics of Quality*, echoes this:
progress is not the result of accumulation,
but the pursuit of refinement—
of deeper meaning and higher awareness.

Growth is not about knowing more.
It is about perceiving more fully—
with perspicuity, ingeniousness, and profoundness.

What you seek is not more knowledge,
but a more expansive way of seeing.

Vygotsky's *Zone of Proximal Development (ZPD)*
furthers this idea:
True growth transpires
not within the bounds of comfort,
but just beyond them—
in that liminal space that challenges us
without undoing us.

Like the body,
the mind adapts to its environment.
Surround it with ease,
repetition, and predictability,
and it will shrink to fit within those confines.
Expose it to challenge,
ambiguity, and complexity,
and it will expand to hold new realities.

This is the paradox of learning:
the more we truly grow,
the more we recognize
how little we know.

Socrates captured this with enduring simplicity:
"The only true wisdom is in knowing
you know nothing."

And the *Dunning-Kruger effect* reminds us:
real understanding begins with humility—
the willingness to recognize
what we do not yet know and
having the courage to confront it.

In the Japanese concept of "no mind" (*mushin)*,
we find another layer of truth:
true mastery begins
where thought falls silent,
when knowing dissolves into
effortless,
intuitive wisdom.

"Be patient toward all that is unsolved in your heart and
try to love the questions themselves,"
said Rainer Maria Rilke.

Growth is not about rushing toward answers,
it is about letting the questions stretch you
before the answers arrive.

For growth is not orderly.
It is messy.
Erratic.
Unpredictable.

And as Ilya Prigogine's
Dissipative Structures theory reveals:
evolution,
whether in systems or in selves,
does not emerge through stability,
but through disruption.

Systems evolve when they are pushed
beyond equilibrium
when they reach critical thresholds,
either collapsing into chaos
or reorganizing into stronger,
more complex,
and adaptive forms.

The same is true for us.

It is not stability that fuels our growth,
but disruption—
moments of
upheaval,
challenge,
and reinvention.

And Hegel's *dialectic* teaches that:
growth is found in
the synthesis of opposites—
thesis and *antithesis*
merging into a higher understanding (*synthesis*).

This synthesis is not
the resolution of opposing forces,
but transformation—
a blossoming of newness.

And as the *Law of Serendipity* suggests,
the most profound transformations
often emerge from the unexpected.

Growth, insight, and discovery arise
from meeting ambiguity
with curiosity
rather than fear.

The shifts in human history,
the deepest moments of personal awakening
were not always the result of direct pursuit,
but of openness to what emerges.

Let us remain open—
curious about what might yet unfold.

For growth is not instantaneous.
It is the slow layering
of choices,
of resilience,
of self-refinement over time.
It is continuous movement—
a mindful cycle of
inquiry,
release,
and renewal.

Relish the discomfort of your growth.

Allow yourself to be changed,
not through monumental leaps,
but in the quiet persistence of becoming.

Each moment you choose to reflect,
each challenge you choose to embrace,
each habit you choose to refine,
each thought you choose to reframe,
designs your becoming.

Honor the process.
Trust its timing.

And one day, without realizing it,
you will look back and see,
you have become the person
you once hoped to be.

Letter 8: Dear Sailor of the Unknown

THE BEAUTY OF UNCERTAINTY

The unknown does not confine you; it is the catalyst for
your transformation—where uncertainty blossoms into
possibility and grants you freedom to become who you
are meant to be.

Uncertainty is not a void.
It is the vast expanse
where dreams are sown,
where brave hearts break new ground.

We are taught to fear the unknown,
to view it as a destructive force that
destabilizes what is secure.

What if uncertainty were not an enemy but an ally?
What if it were instead the rich soil
where vision takes root,
where imagination awakens,
where daring turns the invisible into tangible?

The unknown does not seek to devour you.
It seeks to transform you.

It invites you to create,
to trust in your own resilience,
to celebrate the beauty of
what is beyond the horizon.

The unknown, Albert Einstein wrote, is
"the most beautiful thing we can experience,"
for within it lies the wellspring of curiosity
that ignites discovery.

This truth was known to Lao Tzu:
"If I let go of who I am, I become what I might be."

The release of control is stepping into the eternal—
to be not a captive of what is
but inspired by what might be.

The unknown, then,
becomes a catalyst for change—
a realm where stagnation
gives way to
purposeful motion.

Joseph Campbell saw this
as the essence of the *Hero's Journey:*
the *hero* must leave the familiar world
and venture into the unknown.

It is only by relinquishing certainty that
transformation becomes possible.

Campbell called it the *refusal of the call*:
when we hold onto false security,
while true growth awaits
in the uncharted territory.

In the *Poetics of Space,* Gaston Bachelard writes
that imagination thrives in undefined spaces.
It is within the unknown,
the space of multifarious reverie,
where vision blooms,
creation unfolds,
and the yet-to-be
begins to take form.

Anaximander's *Apeiron*,
the boundless, the inexhaustible,
describes reality as an infinite,
ever-generating source,
from where all things
materialize,
dissolve,
and return.

Limits are not inherent but imposed by perception.

The unknown is not emptiness,
but a continuum,
an open horizon
expanding as far as
we dare to explore.

Zygmunt Bauman captured this reality
in his notion of *Liquid Modernity*:
a world where social structures
no longer solidify,
but remain in constant flux.

Previous generations could build lives
around stable institutions,
but today's reality is characterized
by fluidity and continuous change.

Those most torn by this *liquidity*
suffer the greatest anxiety,
while those who navigate uncertain waters
discover new forms
of resilience and adaptability.

In *liquid* times,
embracing uncertainty
becomes a practical necessity.

What separates a life of desperation
from one of inspired contribution
is not greater certainty,
but greater courage to
move purposefully into
uncertainty's creative space.

For uncertainty is a furnace for creation.
Yet, it demands faith—
in yourself,
in the process of becoming,
in the truth that every unanswered question
holds a promise.

Your mind was designed for exploration.
It evolved not to find comfort,
but to solve,
to seek,
to move forward into the questions that
do not yet have answers.

Psychologists Costa and McCrae found
openness to experience
as the quality most related to
cognitive flexibility
and creativity.

A mind that resists change becomes rigid.
A mind that adapts evolves and thrives.

Heidegger offered us *Gelassenheit*:
a philosophical attitude of
"releasement" or "letting-be"
as an alternative to
our obsessive desire for control.

Instead of seeking certainty,
we are invited to release our grip.
This is not passive resignation,
but active receptivity to the limitless.

The brain seeks closure,
as the *Zeigarnik effect* reveals,
holding onto unfinished narratives
with a sense of urgency.

The unknown unsettles us
because it is unresolved,
demanding completion through
our choices,
our actions,
our will.

Simone de Beauvoir recognized this
in her *Ethics of Ambiguity,*
noting that
human life at its root is ambiguous.

We are at once free yet constrained,
isolated yet connected,
finite yet reaching for infinity.

"Man must not attempt to dispel the ambiguity of his
being," she wrote,
"but accept it and learn to thrive within it."

The rigid mind seeks escape
through absolute certainties and dogmas.
The liberated mind accepts
fundamental uncertainty
as the very condition
for meaningful freedom.

The experience of liminality,
the in-between of what was and what will be,
evokes unease.

Yet it is within this threshold that
our most profound transformations
take place.

In transition,
we are unmade and remade,
woven by the unknown into
what we are becoming.

History turns at the hands of those
who question the contours
of the known and find,
in uncertainty,
the seeds of what's possible.

And so,
accept ambiguity.
For you were not meant
to be stagnant or omniscient,
you were meant to move forward,
to reach beyond the bounds of certainty,
to transform the unknown before you
into a reality only you can create.

The unknown
does not bind you
or hold you back.
It invites you to become
all you aspire to be.

Letter 9: Dear Phoenix

THE SACRED TRANSFORMATION

> *Within the flames that threaten to destroy you, lies your*
> *sacred transformation—burning away the nonessential,*
> *purifying what endures, and creating space for your*
> *authentic self to finally emerge.*

From the ashes of your deepest losses,
you emerge transformed.

Not as a shadow of who you were,
but as someone
deeper, wiser, more resilient,
forged by the fire of adversity.

Life is not a steady,
linear ascent toward some distant summit.

It is a spiral dance of destruction and rebirth,
where each end births a beginning,
each collapse contains creation.

In every burning star,
every dying galaxy,
every collapsing supernova—
creation emerges from destruction.

You are not separate from this cosmic rhythm.

Fire reveals its brilliant contradiction:
what burns you also refines you,
what consumes your past
creates space for your becoming.

The very flames that threaten to destroy you
ultimately illuminate your strength.

Hegel captured this through his
concept of sublation (*Aufhebung*):
true transformation transcends
by preserving what came before.

Your wounds become wisdom.
Your struggles become insight.
Your losses carve space for a life
more honest,
more whole,
more alive.

In Hindu tradition, the sacred fire (*Agni*)
serves as a messenger between worlds—
the physical and the divine,
transforming the old into
something pure and renewed.

Through rebirth,
you transform your pain into growth,
your grief into purpose,
your endings into rebirths.

The *Phoenix effect*,
in post-traumatic growth, reveals that
people emerge from suffering with
expanded compassion,
deeper relationships,
and clearer vision for
what truly matters.

And the *First Law of Thermodynamics*
offers a profound truth:
energy cannot be
created or destroyed,
only transformed from
one form to the other.

What feels like irrevocable loss is
energy changing forms.

You, too, are energy becoming—
never quite the same,
yet always recognizable,
constantly renewed.

In chaos theory, the *Butterfly effect* suggests that
disruption signals not breakdown
but breakthrough—
systems reorganizing themselves
into greater complexity.

You are no exception to this pulse of being.
You are its perfect expression.

Your past has formed you,
but it does not define you.

Rise not to escape your past,
but to fulfill its purpose.

Rise not to become someone else,
but to become who you already are
beneath the disguises.

Your challenges are not punishments or obstacles,
but invitations to emerge as something
more refined,
more authentic,
and more awakened.

The world does not need your perfection,
it needs the light of your transformation.

Letter 10: Dear Keeper of Time

THE PHILOSOPHY OF ENOUGH

*The greatest freedom is not having more time—it is
liberating yourself from the tyranny of seeing time as
something outside yourself that you are constantly
racing against.*

We measure our days in numbers—
hours spent,
deadlines met,
tasks completed.

We chase the illusion that
more time,
more achievement,
more accumulation,
will finally grant us peace.

But what if fulfillment is not found in more,
but in the quiet realization that
we have already enough?

Time has never been the enemy.
The real enemy is the belief that
we must do more to be worthy of it.

Zhuangzi taught that:
peace is found not in controlling the river,
but in becoming like an empty boat upon it.

Life moves as it will—
to resist is to struggle,
to let go is to
move with the current.

Surrendering to its rhythm
allows us to flow freely,
unburdened by resistance.

As St. Augustine reflected,
the past exists only in memory,
the future only in expectation,
and the present is so fleeting that
it barely exists
before slipping into the past.

Yet we anchor ourselves in what was,
and exhaust ourselves chasing
what has yet to be,
forgetting that
the only time
we truly inhabit is
now.

As Heidegger once said,
we do not exist *in* time,
we exist *as* time.

Most people, he argues,
live in *inauthentic time*,
reacting to events,
following societal scripts,
avoiding deeper reflection.

To live authentically is to
awaken to our finitude,
to stop outsourcing meaning to the future,
to take full responsibility
for our own becoming.

The way we relate to
the past,
the present,
and the future
defines who we are.

As Zeno's paradoxes remind us,
motion itself is an illusion,
as is our pursuit of "more time"
Time is not something to accumulate.
It is only ever encountered in the present.

Bergson's concept of *duration (durée)*
reframes time—
not as a measurable, linear sequence,
but as a qualitative, conscious experience.

The more present we are,
the more time expands.
The more we rush,
the more it contracts.

To be at peace with time
is to recognize that the only moment
ever truly ours
is this one.

Yet the world tells us otherwise.

Comparison culture warps our perception of time,
convincing us that we are behind,
that we must catch up,
that success is a race
we are already losing.

Capitalism thrives on dissatisfaction—
on convincing us that we are incomplete,
that happiness exists somewhere in the future,
waiting behind the next achievement.

Hustle culture venerates exhaustion,
treating rest as laziness and
ambition as the ultimate virtue.
To be still is to be unproductive
and to be unproductive is to be left behind.

Social media creates an illusion of scarcity—
of time, of success, of opportunity—
filling our minds with comparisons,
insinuating that we are late,
that we are missing something essential.

The *Hedonic Treadmill effect* echoes this trap:
no matter how much we achieve,
accumulate, or attain,
satisfaction fades,
and we find ourselves running toward the next thing,
and then the next, and the next,
until life itself becomes
a mirage of deferred arrival,
always just out of reach.

But what if arrival is not a place we must reach,
but a moment we must claim?
What if time is not something to maximize,
but something to savor?
What if the answer is not more, but enough?

The world does not teach us how to be content.
It teaches us how to chase.

Albert Camus wrote:
"Real generosity toward the future
lies in giving all to the present."

You do not need to rush.
You do not need to chase.
You do not need to force urgency into your being.

Give yourself fully—
to this breath,
to this sunset,
to this version of yourself.

You are not falling behind.
You are not running out of time.
You are exactly where you are meant to be.

And that is enough.
This moment—
already whole,
already beautiful,
already yours.

Letter 11: Dear Keeper of Balance

THE DANCE OF DUALITIES

*Balance is not a fixed state, but a dynamic dance
between opposites, where each rise and fall,
each expansion and contraction, shapes you into who
you are becoming.*

Life is not about eliminating extremes.
It is about mastering the sacred dance between them.

True fulfillment does not arise from avoiding tension,
but from embracing the unity of opposites—
where seemingly contradictory forces,
create something greater than
the sum of their parts.

Just as the inhale cannot exist without the exhale,
our capacity for transformation depends on
our willingness to both
disrupt and stabilize,
advance and retreat,
at precisely
the right moments.

Too often, we fragment our experience,
compressing life's richness into false binaries.

Yet the most vivid life is lived
in the tension that creates
the full spectrum of
our humanity.

Balance is not a fixed state,
but a continuous adjustment process
within all living systems.

It calls for developing enough inner complexity
to respond fluidly to life's evolving demands.

Balance is not about perfect equilibrium,
but about navigating the creative friction
between apparent opposites:
structure and spontaneity,
discipline and freedom,
ambition and acceptance,
connection and solitude.

When structure is overemphasized,
it calcifies into rigidity.
When spontaneity is left unchecked,
it dissolves into formlessness.

When ambition dominates,
it spirals into restlessness or burnout.
When acceptance is taken too far,
it drifts into complacency or stagnation.
When connection is over-pursued,
it blurs boundaries and depletes the self.
When solitude becomes isolation,
it erodes the very sense of belonging we seek.

When we learn to honor
both sides of these polarities,
rather than clinging to one,
we open ourselves to
a more profound experience.

Simone Weil said:
"Harmony is the balance of opposites,
a truth that reflects the nature of reality itself."

This balance is not merely the absence of conflict.
It is power—
to create,
to stand still in the whirlwind
without being consumed by it,
to navigate life's extremes
with ferocity and grace.

The *Tao Te Ching* illuminates this wisdom:
"There is a time for being ahead,
a time for being behind,
a time for being in motion,
a time for being at rest."

Nature thrives not in stasis,
but in rhythmic oscillation—
the innate intelligence of cycles that
guide all life.

Just as the seasons turn,
just as night follows day,
we too must learn
when to move forward,
when to be still,
when to persist, and
when to let go.

Our bodies, too,
thrive not in fixed states,
but through constant adaptation—
contracting and relaxing,
warming and cooling,
taking in and releasing.

Vitality, after all,
does not come from constant striving,
but from rhythm

The ancient Greeks recognized *enantiodromia*:
that everything, in time, transforms into its opposite.
The zenith of order gives birth to chaos.
The nadir of darkness summons light.

Yet in much of Western thinking,
opposites are not held in tension,
but ranked—
success above failure,
work above rest,
certainty above doubt.

Ancient philosophies across cultures
honor the integration of opposites—
a wisdom that transcends either/or thinking
and moves toward wholeness
beyond fragmentation.

This is the "middle way"—
not compromise,
but transcendence,
where the marriage of opposites
catalyzes evolutionary leaps.

The dance between opposites
is not a problem to solve.
It is the essence of a fully lived life.

Trust the dance. Trust the rhythm. Trust yourself.

When you embrace
the full spectrum of experience,
light and shadow,
certainty and doubt,
expansion and contraction,
you do not merely achieve balance.
You become it.

You embody it,
not as a fixed state,
but as motion attuned to harmony.

And in that attunement,
you begin to move not against life,
but with it.

Move with the rhythm that
created stars and oceans.
Trust its wisdom.

For in the silence between seasons,
each rise and fall,
each expansion and contraction,
you are not just enduring,
you are becoming.

PART III:

THE ART *of* ALIGNMENT

Letter 12: Dear Trustor

THE QUIET UPRISING OF SELF-TRUST

> *Self-trust is not about blind optimism or avoiding risk.*
> *It is the courageous commitment to take a leap of*
> *faith—an act of trust placed in something not yet fully*
> *seen or proven.*

To trust yourself is to reclaim your power—
an act of alignment,
not arrogance.

It is to honor the inner strength within you,
the unshakable knowing that
within you lies the wisdom
to chart your own course,
to make decisions anchored in your truth,
and to stand firm even
when the world
tells you otherwise.

As Ralph Waldo Emerson wrote,
"Trust thyself: every heart vibrates to that iron string."

In that vibration,
you find the resonance
of your true potential.

Self-trust is not gifted at birth.
It is a progressive achievement,
tempered by experiences of
both confidence and vulnerability.

Every time you honor
a commitment to yourself,
you strengthen the neural architecture that
underlies your beliefs in
trust,
self-respect,
and resilience.

Every time you align
your actions with your values,
despite discomfort,
you reinforce the belief
in your ability to
act with purpose,
honor your commitment,
and live with intention.

This is how trust becomes embodied,
not merely understood,
but lived.
Felt.
Integrated

We live in a world designed to disconnect us
from our own wisdom.

The journey back to self-trust
begins with recognizing
how much of this external programming,
we have internalized.

Those critical inner voices,
those anxious hesitations,
those persistent doubts,
they are not yours.

They are echoes of past criticism,
projected fears,
and societal expectations
you have absorbed along the way.

To trust yourself is to take ownership of your life—
to choose your own voice over
the chorus of external opinions.

To move forward even in the presence of fear,
to affirm that every decision—right or wrong—
is yours to make,
yours to learn from,
and yours to carry.

Self-trust requires awareness,
recognizing the personas we adopt
to meet external expectations—
the masks we wear that
gradually silence our authentic voice.

We sculpt ourselves to belong,
but in the process,
we often abandon the very voice that
knows where we're meant to go.

To return to that voice,
we must reclaim inner space—
creating pauses
between stimulus and response,
moments of stillness where we can feel
what is true beneath the noise.

When we listen within,
we are tuning into bodily sensations that
signal meaning before the mind has found the words.

This is the *felt sense*:
a holistic, embodied awareness
that holds implicit knowing,
not yet verbalized,
but deeply known.

To access this inner compass,
we develop *interoception*:
the capacity to accurately perceive
our internal states—
the warmth that signals alignment,
the constriction that warns misdirection.

Self-trust is not blind optimism,
nor is it the avoidance of risk.

As Søren Kierkegaard wrote,
it is the courageous commitment to
take a *leap of faith*—
an act of trust placed in something
not yet visible or proven.

Each decision you make,
no matter how small,
carves your path,
refines your vision,
and fortifies your foundation.

The path does not appear before the step,
it appears because of it.

Self-trust does not reject external input.
It is an act of *differentiation*:
the ability to consider the voices around you
without being ruled by them.
It is the daily practice of
discerning which desires
align with your deepest values.

The deepest regrets often come
not from failure,
but from betraying
what you knew to be true
in order to conform.

What haunts us is not falling short,
but the unlived life—
the path we never took
because we silenced the voice within.

When you do not trust yourself,
you give your power away—
to others, to circumstances,
to fear itself.
And in doing so,
you disconnect
from the brilliance within you.

Self-trust is not built in overt declarations,
but through ordinary acts of alignment
repeated over time.

The world does not need more people
who blindly follow conventional wisdom.
It needs more people who have the courage
to listen inward,
to bring forth the gifts only they can offer,
to walk paths that have not yet been walked,
and to live from genuine conviction
instead of dissolving into
the safety of consensus.

Your life belongs to you.
No external authority holds
the unique constellation of your
experiences,
perspectives,
and inner truths.

For somewhere within you
lives the memory of
who you were,
before the world told you
who to be.

With every choice that
honors your truth,
your clarity sharpens,
your presence expands,
and your path becomes
unmistakeably your own.

Carl Jung wrote:
"Your vision will become clear only
when you look into your own heart.
Who looks outside, dreams;
who looks inside, awakens."

Trust in your leap.
Trust in yourself.

For it is in this trust that
your journey will take form,
revealing not only the way forward,
but the full magnitude
of who you are becoming.

Letter 13: Dear Keeper of Integrity

THE COMPASS WITHIN

Integrity is not about perfection—it is about wholeness.
The word itself comes from "integer,"
meaning complete, undivided.

Integrity is more than honesty.
It is the alignment between
your actions and your innermost truth—
a fidelity to what is right,
even when no one is watching,
even when the cost is high.

It is not performance,
but principle.
Not compliance,
but conviction.

To live with integrity
is to be anchored in what matters most—
to honor your values
even when the world rewards betrayal,
to remain whole
where others fracture for approval.

Kant spoke of this in his *categorical imperative*:
"Could I will my action to become universal law?"

Integrity answers not in theory,
but in how you live.

It is a lived ethic—
a promise to yourself
that you will not act in ways
you would condemn in another.

Living this imperative means
creating a world where,
if all followed suit,
justice would naturally flourish.

To choose integrity is to live as if
every act sets a precedent
for the world you are building.
It is choosing
meaning over ease,
substance over surface,
depth over display.

It is the refusal to fragment the self—
to be one person in public
and another in solitude.

Integrity is integration—
the weaving together of every part of you
into a single, undivided whole.

The word itself comes from *integer*:
to be complete, to be unbroken.
It is the resistance to fracture yourself
to meet expectation or to flee discomfort.
It is the art of being someone you can trust—
a self that is unified,
fully expressed,
and deeply aligned.

Plato called this inner harmony as *kalon*:
a beauty that transcends appearance,
rooted in the soul's alignment with virtue.
This is not the beauty of perfection,
but the radiance of congruence
when what you believe, feel, and do
move as one.

Cicero called it *officium*:
the duty you owe not only to others,
but to yourself.
He knew that
the truest test of character
is how you act when no one sees.

Virtue is not submission to rules out of fear,
but discipline born of reverence—
a devotion to the right,
simply because it is right.

Integrity does not demand flawlessness.
It calls for practical wisdom—
the ability to discern,
to admit when you are wrong,
and to begin again in truth.

When Socrates stood before his accusers,
he chose death over disavowal of his convictions.
"The unexamined life is not worth living," he said,
not as theory,
but as a life embodied.

His sacrifice was not for reputation,
but for coherence—
for the immovable truth within him.

In an age of calculation,
where metrics replace meaning
and compromise wears the mask of strategy,
integrity becomes a radical stand—
a choice to remain whole
in a broken world.

Aristotle called the fruit of
this choice *eudaimonia*:
not fleeting pleasure,
but a flourishing that endures
through every season.

"Waste no more time arguing what a good man should
be. Be one," urged Marcus Aurelius—
a reminder that character
is not proclaimed,
but proven.

This fractured world
does not need
more spectacle,
more brilliance,
more cleverly disguised compromise.

It needs people who refuse to trade
their truth for applause.
Who measure success
not by what they gain,
but by what they refuse to lose.

Integrity is the one thing no one can steal.
You can only surrender it,
willingly.

In a world of shifting tides,
to stand in your wholeness
is the ultimate act of self-respect.

This is both your inheritance and your offering.
To be the rare soul who can say:
"This is who I am, in darkness and in light."
"This is the truth I serve."
"This is the line I will not cross."

And to mean it.

Letter 14: Dear Authentic Self

THE ECHO OF TRUTH

*Authenticity is an ongoing, radical act of creation—
a love story between you and the self you are still
uncovering.*

In a world that constantly urges you
to fit,
to shrink,
to mold yourself into something palatable,
authenticity becomes an act of defiance.

It is the refusal to be a construct of expectation.
It is the reclamation of your own becoming—
a shedding of conditioned layers,
allowing your essence to rise
through your chosen truth,
not one imposed.

Authenticity is not an aesthetic
nor a carefully curated identity.
It is the audacity to stand unarmored
in the raw truth
of who you are.

Jean-Paul Sartre named its opposite
mauvaise foi—bad faith:
the self-deception of trading your freedom
for the safety of a borrowed self,
for the illusion of belonging
at the cost of being.

To live authentically
is to reject the false equivalence
between validation and security.

It is to embrace uncertainty,
to stand at the crossroads
of fact and possibility,
and to choose,
always,
your own truth.

Hegel called it the struggle for recognition
(Kampf um Anerkennung).
The self is not born in isolation,
but forged in the sacred space
of being truly seen.

Yet recognition must not be won through imitation,
but through the unflinching expression of your truth.

As bell hooks wrote:
"The moment we choose to love,
we begin to move against domination,
against oppression."

Authenticity is not self-expression for applause,
it is self-liberation.

It is not a war against the world,
but a refusal to be consumed by it,
to lose yourself in the name of connection.

Martin Buber spoke of the *I-Thou relationship*:
those rare, profound encounters
where we meet each other
beyond roles, beyond expectations.

In these sacred moments,
authenticity is not only found,
it is mirrored.

We fear rejection as proof of inadequacy,
tying our worth to the whims of approval.

Yet, as Alain de Botton reminds us:
rejection is not a verdict.
It is clarity.

It does not diminish who we are,
it simply reveals
where your truth diverges from
the world's expectations.

And in that knowing,
true resilience is born.
Your worth does not waver
in the face of disapproval.

Simone de Beauvoir teaches us:
freedom is not the absence of uncertainty,
but the courage to engage with it.

Authenticity does not promise ease,
it promises wholeness.
It may ask you to stand alone,
to honor your integrity,
when applause is absent
and exile is near.

Even rejection
can become a rite of passage.

To say no to what diminishes you
is to say yes to everything that honors you.

Selfhood is not inherent.
It is a battle—
a cycle of unmaking and remaking.

First, the unraveling:
the peeling back of roles,
masks,
beliefs never truly yours.

Then, the becoming:
the deliberate, devoted creation
of a life that reflects
who you are beneath it all.

Authenticity is not rigidity,
it is resonance between
what you believe and how you live.

It is the unshakable decision
to exist as you are,
not as the world expects you to be.

It is an ongoing, radical commitment
to live in alignment,
to exist without apology,
and to honor the self
you are still uncovering.

You are not a mask to be worn
nor a shadow to be disowned.

Stand in the truth you form—
unshaken by applause,
unmoved by dismissal.

For authenticity needs
no permission,
no audience,
no validation.

It simply thrives—
in truth,
in wholeness,
in the unwavering grace
of being
unapologetically yourself.

Letter 15: Dear Lover of The Self

THE PHILOSOPHY OF SELF-LOVE

Self-love is not the glorified selfishness our culture fears, but the essential foundation from which all genuine connection grows.

Self-love is not selfishness.
It is the quiet root
from which all else grows:
every connection you attract,
every vision you create,
every truth you dare to become.

It is not indulgence,
but alignment—
a remembrance that
you are worthy
not because of what you do,
but because of who you are.

Without this foundation,
every achievement becomes an echo in emptiness,
every relationship, a transaction,
and every purpose,
not an expression of essence,
but a plea for your worth.

Buddhist thought teaches:
self-compassion is the doorway to enlightenment.

To love yourself is to offer
the same boundless kindness,
the same gentle grace,
that you would extend to a dear friend
in their most fragile hour.

Karuna—compassion,
and *metta*—loving-kindness,
are not optional virtues,
they are the very ground of presence.

They ask us to meet ourselves
not with judgment,
but with tenderness.

Yet we have been taught the opposite—
that criticism builds character,
that harshness hones ambition,
that softness is weakness.

A culture of self-neglect convinces us
that greatness is born of self-denial,
that we must diminish ourselves
to be worthy of rising.

But both research and lived experience
reveal the truth:
It is self-compassion, not self-judgment,
that breeds resilience.
It is self-acceptance, not self-criticism,
that sustains growth.

To love yourself
is not to claim perfection,
but to honor your humanity
while choosing to keep becoming.

Your relationship with yourself
becomes the blueprint
for every bond you form.

If you believe you are not enough,
you will approach love through
the lens of performance—
proving, pleasing, perfecting.

But when you stand in your worth,
you create space for love
rooted in mutual respect,
and the beauty of being wholly seen.

Spinoza once wrote that
true freedom comes from understanding—
in seeing yourself as an inseparable part
of nature's whole.

To see yourself not as other,
but as belonging,
not apart from the world,
but arising within it.

The most liberating truth lies in knowing:
the voices that question your worth
were never truly yours.

They were planted by
a culture that profits
from your self-doubt,
and thrives when you forget
your wholeness.

To recognize these voices as foreign
is the first act of your inner revolution—
of reclaiming your freedom.

Self-love is a returning—
to patience,
presence,
and gentleness.

It is the subtle bravery
of sitting with your pain
rather than silencing it,
allowing it to soften
in the light of your attention.

It is the tender act
of listening to your needs without judgment,
honoring them not as inconveniences,
but as reflections of your inner truth.

It is offering yourself love.
Not as a reward for perfection,
nor as a prize for performance,
but as an affirmation of your being.

This is the path of healing:
not loud, not linear,
but honest—
and wholly yours.

The parts you have hidden—
your tenderness,
your rigor,
your questions,
your cracks you have tried to seal—
are not flaws to overcome,
nor burdens to bear in silence.

They are facets of your humanity,
longing to be seen,
to be held with love.
For it is in embracing
what you once concealed
that you begin to live not in fragments,
but in wholeness.

To practice self-love
is not self-absorption.
It is the courage of
becoming intimately aware of yourself,
and meeting that awareness
with kindness.

It is not self-centeredness,
but a return to your own center—
the inner axis
from which integrity and alignment grow.

It is the unblemished discipline
of turning inward,
not to retreat from life,
but to listen to what aches,
to tend to what has long been neglected,
and to offer yourself the healing
that only presence can bring.

The greatest misconception
is that self-love is a feeling—
something you have or lack.

But it is not.
It is a devotion.
A decision—
to speak with respect,
to forgive without condition,
to honor your boundaries,
to remain loyal to your truth
even when the world tempts you to abandon it.

For your capacity to love others
will never exceed your capacity to love yourself.

Not because self-love matters more,
but because you cannot give
what you do not have.

You cannot recognize beauty in others
if you have been taught to deny it in yourself.
You cannot offer genuine connection
while starving for it within.

When you know your worth,
you no longer chase love,
you radiate it.
You no longer reach for belonging,
you start resting in its presence within.

This is the power of self-love:
not that it centers you above others,
but that it centers you within yourself.

And so, love yourself—
fiercely, gently, without apology.

Let that love be the wellspring of your joy,
the root of your peace,
and the enduring source of your strength.

And as you walk this path,
steadfast in your truth,
know that you do not need to be anything
other than who you are, right now,
to be worthy of love—your own, and the world's.

Letter 16: Dear Lover of Life

THE PHILOSOPHY OF LOVING LIFE

To love life is not to mourn its passing, but to cherish it precisely because it is finite—to see each moment as something arriving fully, fleetingly, magnificently—never to be repeated in the same way again.

To love life is to witness it—
not to control it,
possess it,
or solve it like a riddle,
but to behold it as sacred,
as fleeting.

It is to bow before impermanence—
not in despair,
but in devotion.

Albert Schweitzer called this *reverence for life*:
the profound recognition that all living beings,
from the softest leaf to the furthest star,
carry within them
the will to exist.

To love life fully
is to walk through the world
with tenderness and responsibility—
to feel, deeply,
that existence itself is a blessing.

It is to see the ordinary as miraculous,
to greet each moment as sacred,
and to act with compassion—
not only toward humanity,
but toward all that lives
and longs to be.

Rabindranath Tagore called it
a *cosmic drama, a divine play (Lila)*:
an unfolding without beginning or end,
where every moment is an invitation
to wonder,
to create,
to surrender.

The river does not resist its passage to the sea.
The flame does not mourn as it flickers and fades.

To love life is to move with it.
To relinquish not as defeat,
but as celebration of its rhythm.

It is to engage with open hands,
not with fear,
but with awe.

The Japanese speak of *mono no aware*:
the gentle ache of impermanence.
The cherry blossom is precious
not despite its fall,
but because of it.
Music moves us because it fades.
Each note,
each petal,
each moment
made luminous by its vanishing.

To love life
is not to mourn its passing,
but to cherish it because it passes.

To see each moment
not as slipping away,
but as arriving—
fully,
fleetingly,
magnificently—
never to return
in quite the same way.

To love life is to embrace its duality.

To love
is to stand at the trembling edge of loss.
To dream
is to risk the ache of falling short.
To live fully
is to offer yourself unguarded—
to wonder and wound,
to joy and sorrow,
to the ecstasy of becoming
and the ache of shedding
what no longer serves.

For the vastness of life
cannot be grasped with clenched fists.
It asks to be held
with open hands,
with a heart tender enough to fracture,
and strong enough to grow
through the cracks.

Albert Camus wrote:
"In the midst of winter,
I found there was,
within me,
an invincible summer."

To love life
is to hold onto that summer,
even in the coldest seasons.

It is the courage to meet
each day,
each moment,
as an unrepeatable gift.

To seek meaning not in perfection,
but in persistence—
not in life's gifts,
but in your giving.

To love life is to immerse yourself in it—
fully,
fearlessly,
without reserve.

Not as a spectator, but as a participant.
Not in resistance, but in surrender.
Not in waiting for the perfect moment,
but in recognition that this moment
—right now—is life itself,
waiting to be lived.

And so,
love life.

Love its flow,
its ebb,
its glow.

Hold it lightly,
yet love it fully.

And in loving life,
become life itself—
unbound,
luminous,
endlessly becoming.

Letter 17: Dear Artist of Gratitude

THE POWER OF GRATITUDE

*Gratitude is not a passive but an active perception—a
deliberate redirection of awareness that reveals the
extraordinary within the ordinary,
seeing life through the eyes of wonder.*

Gratitude is not a sentiment.
It is a way of being—
a shift in perception
that transforms the ordinary into sacred.

It is to meet life not with entitlement,
but with adoration—
to recognize each moment
not as something owed,
but as something offered.

This is where transformation begins—
in the soft undoing of our ancient negativity bias,
once essential for survival,
now dimming our vision,
replacing presence with absence,
abundance with scarcity.

To give thanks
is to affirm what sustains us—
the unseen efforts,
the quiet workings of grace,
the blessings that arrive
without announcement,

It is to move in harmony with existence,
knowing that giving and receiving
are not opposites,
but currents of the same river.

We are not masters of life,
nor authors of its unfolding,
but receivers and givers
in equal measure.

Like *wu wei*,
the Taoist art of effortless action,
gratitude is a yielding born of trust.

Not resignation,
but recognition
of life's deeper flow.

Modern life teaches
that abundance lies in accumulation.

Yet gratitude reveals a deeper truth:
abundance dwells not in what you own,
but how you see.

True wealth is found in
the *beginner's mind* (*shoshin*):
the capacity to greet each moment
with renewed presence,
to witness the miraculous within the mundane,
to remain open to wonder
where others see routine.

We chase marvels across continents,
yet overlook the miracle of breath,
the gift of this very moment.

Arigatai teaches that gratitude
encompasses all that life offers—
not only joy,
but hardship,
impermanence,
and the unseen undercurrents of life.

Gratitude does not separate
gain from loss,
light from shadow.
It honors them both
as essential parts of the whole.

And yet,
we often postpone our appreciation,
telling ourselves,
"I will be grateful when things change."

In doing so,
we defer fulfillment indefinitely,
trapped in an endless cycle
of striving without arrival.

Radical gratitude is *amor fati*:
a love of fate,
an embrace of life as it is,
even in its difficulty.

It sees adversity not as detour,
but as gateway.
Not as punishment,
but as a necessary crossing.

It is meeting the moment
without adornment—
through the simple act of attention,
the remembrance of all that is already here:
the miracle of consciousness,
the sheer unlikelihood
of our very existence.

Appreciation knows no bounds.
The mind becomes what it beholds,
constantly reshaped
by the attention you offer.

To be grateful
is to wake up from the illusion
that life is something to control,
rather than receive.

Through gratitude,
you do not move through time,
you expand within it.

Rooted in the present,
you honor the past,
and welcome the future
not with fear,
but with trust.

In this sacred attention,
nothing is too small to be seen.

Live fully.
Feel what was,
what is,
and what will be—
as one:
a singular,
unrepeatable,
gift.

Letter 18: Dear Mirror Gazer

THE REFLECTION OF THE SELF & THE OTHER

*Relationships reveal both who we are and the risk of
seeing ourselves through fractured lenses. Living
authentically in relationships means recognizing the
distinction between genuine reflections and projections
of others' fears and insecurities.*

Every relationship is a mirror.

To stand before another
is to witness both light and shadow—
what you know of yourself,
and what still remains hidden.

It is within relationships
that we are most fully revealed,
not as isolated beings,
but as ones
shaped,
softened,
and sharpened
by the presence of another.

Martin Buber spoke of two ways to relate:
I-It and I-Thou.

In I-It,
we reduce the other to a function,
a role,
a means to an end.

But in I-Thou,
we meet them as they are,
not as a projection of our desires,
not as props of our own story,
but as souls standing in their own right—
sovereign,
whole.

To love fully,
to connect deeply,
is to meet another in this sacred space.

To honor their being
without molding it
to fit our expectations
and in doing so,
to encounter more of our own.

Jean-Paul Sartre believed that
we come to know ourselves
through how we are perceived.

Yet mirrors do more than reveal.
They also distort.

Perception is never pure.
It is colored by wounds,
fears, and unspoken histories.

The danger is mistaking the mirror for truth,
believing that how someone sees you
defines who you are.

To live authentically in relationships
is to discern the difference
between genuine reflection
and mere projection.

It is about discerning when the mirror
reveals an aspect of yourself,
and when it reflects another's narrative onto you.

Thich Nhat Hanh's concept of *interbeing*,
reminds us that we do not exist in isolation.

Just as the moon does not shine without the sun,
we do not fully see ourselves
without the presence of others.

And yet,
while others reflect us,
they do not complete us.

The idea of the "other half"
is a beautiful myth
as if we were born incomplete,
awaiting another
to make us whole.

Love was never meant to fill a void.
It was always meant to magnify
what is already whole within us.

True love is not about completion,
but expansion and alignment.
Not about merging,
but growing in parallel motion,
rooted in shared values,
and dreaming toward the same horizon.

It is the synchronicity of vision—
dreams we carry now,
and the ones we dare
to imagine together.

Dreams that do not compete but converge.
Each purpose made more radiant
in the light of the other's.

It is a symphony of energies—
fluid,
respectful,
empowering.
Where love is not possession,
but presence.
Not dependence,
but wholehearted devotion.

As Kahlil Gibran wrote:
"Let there be spaces
in your togetherness,
and let the winds of the heavens
dance between you."

True love does not dissolve the self.
It deepens it.

You do not lose yourself in the other.
You discover new dimensions
in their gaze,
their voice,
their unwavering belief in you.

It is liberation in togetherness,
a safe haven
where both can unfold fully,
seen in their wholeness,
held in their becoming,
and celebrated for all that they are
and all they are still growing into.

A love that does not confine,
but amplifies.

It is not just the building of a shared life,
but the creation of a shared inner world—
a sanctuary of reverence,
where every glance is a homecoming,
and every challenge,
an invitation to grow closer.

This kind of love is rare.

Not because it is impossible,
but because it requires
presence,
intention,
and the courage to be truly seen.

Yet not all mirrors are kind.
Some reflect what we would rather not face—
our fears,
our insecurities,
the habits we have not yet released.

Carl Jung called this the *shadow self*:
the parts we hide,
yet unknowingly offer
in our interactions with others.

When conflict arises,
it is tempting to blame the mirror—
to accuse, to retreat, to project.

But the deeper question is not,
"What is this relationship revealing about them?",
but rather,
"What is it revealing about me?"

Even tension carries wisdom.
Those who trigger us
often illuminate unhealed wounds.
Those who frustrate us
may reflect the parts of ourselves
we have not yet learned to love.

Growth in relationships
does not come from reshaping others.
It comes from allowing their reflection
to catalyze our own transformation.

For relationships are not just about companionship.

Every person offers a different mirror:
some will show your light.
some will expose your shadow.
some will distort your reflection
through the fractures of their own pain.

But among all these reflections,
one holds true:
your own.

When relationships shift,
when mirrors change,
when all else fades,
you are left with the self you have cultivated:
the wisdom you have gained,
the love you have learned to give,
the truth you have learned to hold,
the grace you have offered—
to others,
and to yourself.

So do not fear what relationships reveal.
Do not turn away from what they teach.
For in the gaze of the other,
you do not merely see them—
you see yourself.

And in truly seeing yourself,
you begin to understand
what it means
to love,
to grow,
to become.

PART IV:

VISION, PURPOSE, AND THE LEGACY *of* IMPACT

Letter 19: Dear Dreamer of Greatness

WALKING ON A DREAM

The dreamers who change the world do not just wish, they declare that what exists today is not all that will ever be, for the greatest tragedy is not failure but the dream unlived, the vision unpursued.

To dream is to defy conformity—
a bold insistence that
what is not yet real
can—and must—
come to life.

Not a retreat from reality,
but a rebellion against its boundaries—
a refusal to inherit a world
you never chose to shape.

To dream is to shatter the quiet consensus
that this—only this—is all there is.

Sartre's *freedom* is not the right to imagine,
but the courage
to act on that imagination.

For to envision a world and then abandon it
is to betray not only the dream,
but the dreamer.

Dreaming is a decision:
a revolt against inertia,
a threshold where vision demands motion.

William Blake called imagination
"the divine body in every man":
the sacred force animating all creation,
revealing the infinite
through the finite.

Dreams are not escapes,
but awakenings—
piercing illusion to witness life
as it longs to be lived:
limitless,
electric,
unfolding.

Your vision is not a solitary spark,
but a radiant force—
one that redraws
not only your path,
but the map of our collective future.

Nietzsche saw dreams as Apollonian grace:
an artistic impulse
that overlays chaos
with symmetry and beauty,
redeeming existence through form.

Kant called dreams involuntary poetry
(unwillkührliches dichten):
images stirred from within,
so vivid they rival the truths of waking life.

In that space,
we do not just imagine,
we become.

In vision,
we overcome the void.
We give shape to the formless
and meaning to the uncertain.

And yet Zhuangzi's *butterfly dream* asks:
can we truly know
where dreaming ends
and waking begins?

Who's to say reality is more valid
than the world we dare to imagine?

Dreamers of greatness do not merely dream,
they refuse the finality of the present.

To dream greatly is to declare:
what is is not all that shall ever be.

The tragedy is not failure.
It is the failure to begin,
letting the world convince you
you are not enough
to carry the vision
only you can see.

But you are.
You always were.

Dreams do not die from lack of worth.
They perish under the illusion of limitation.

To dream is to participate
in humanity's oldest ritual:
calling forth the unseen
through belief,
through breath,
through action.

To walk on your dream
is to move with courage—
to remain loyal to a vision
before it even wears a name.

Your dream needs no permission.
Only your devotion,
your momentum,
your leap into the unseen.

This journey reshapes
more than the world around you.
It reshapes you.

As you manifest your vision,
you become the one
your vision has always summoned—
resilient in trials,
wise in unfolding,
aligned with what's true.

Here,
you discover purpose—
where action flows from essence,
and belief finds its form.

And in walking on your dream,
you become worthy
of bringing it to life.

And so,
honor your dream.
Protect it.
Pursue it with fire.

Let your dream remind you:
life is not about yielding to what is,
but stretching toward
what could be.

It exists for your becoming—
more whole,
more aware,
more true to the voice within.

For the dream is not only
what you build,
but who you become
in the sacred act
of walking on it.

Letter 20: Dear Pioneer

FORGING NEW FRONTIERS

All pioneers begin their journeys with questioning.
Instead of accepting conventional wisdom about what's
realistic or practical, they begin to see these 'realities'
as constructed narratives that can be reimagined.

To pioneer is to act,
not for rebellion's sake,
but in devotion to a vision that
goes beyond the present and
dares to reimagine what is possible.

It is not the abandonment of reason,
but the integration of reason and instinct—
a trust in their gentle confluence.

Friedrich Schiller called this *aesthetic freedom:*
where creativity becomes the bridge
between impulse and discipline,
liberating the self from rigidity,
and allowing reality to be composed
with intention and grace.

Yet the path of the pioneer is never one of ease.

Hannah Arendt's *natality* reminds us:
to begin is a radical act—
an interruption,
a disruption,
a declaration that the world
can be made new.

To pioneer is to become
an agent of this renewal—
to step beyond the known
not for escape,
but to expand the horizon of human possibility.

For the greatest frontier
are not drawn in maps,
but in minds.

We all carry invisible frameworks
assumptions inherited,
limits disguised as norms—
shaped by culture, education,
and the narratives we were never taught to question.

All pioneers begin their journeys with inquiry.
Not just how to solve a problem,
but whether the problem itself
is framed correctly.

Pioneering begins where consensus ends,
when you stop asking what is allowed,
and start asking what is true.

For the boldest form of innovation
is not always invention,
but reimagining the lens itself:
the mental models,
the systems of meaning,
the structures of thought.

It is the courage to ask:
Who gets to define the frontiers?
Whose vision is legitimized?
Whose boundaries are recognized?

A pioneer does not wait for approval.
A pioneer does not ask permission.
A pioneer steps forward
because the future demands it.

To pioneer is to choose:
conscience over comfort,
conviction over convention,
truth over tradition.

Every system resists change.
It is designed to preserve itself
and that resistance is not random.
It is the natural friction of transformation
pressing against what longs
to remain unchanged.

The tension you feel is not failure,
it is impact—
evidence that your disruption is real.

Pioneering lives in paradox:
a fusion of vision and discipline,
of dreaming wide
and delivering precisely—
where creativity diverges
and will converges.

Thoreau understood this:
progress demands resistance—
the refusal to accept
what diminishes us
as inevitable.

Heraclitus wrote:
panta rhei—
everything flows.
Nothing is fixed.
Existence itself is a current of becoming.

The pioneer is the catalyst—
a spark in the current,
an architect of evolution.

The pioneer's journey is not only personal.
It is ancestral.
It is spiritual.

To pioneer is to participate
in the long unfolding
of consciousness and culture.

Change comes not through recklessness,
but through courageous clarity:
the steadiness of vision,
and the conviction to build
what does not yet exist.

Anaïs Nin once wrote,
"Life shrinks or expands in proportion
to one's courage."

And indeed—
courage is the seed of
every turning point.

The future does not belong to the cautious.
It belongs to those who dare —
to imagine wildly,
to speak fiercely,
to act boldly
in the face of resistance.

To pioneer is not merely to forge ahead.
It is to lead with awakened presence.
To walk not with bravado,
but with grounded courage.

For something within you refuses to settle.
Something within you knows:
the horizon was never meant to be admired,
it was always meant to be crossed.

Letter 21: Dear Architect of Legacy

THE IMPRINT YOU LEAVE

*The architecture of your life, this magnificent structure
you are creating moment by moment, is the most
important work you will ever do, not just for yourself
but for the world you briefly inhabit and permanently
influence.*

To live with purpose is not merely to exist.
It is to create something enduring.
It is to shape a life
whose echo outlasts ambition,
whose architecture stands long after
the moment has passed.

You are not a passive figure
swept along by circumstance.
You are a deliberate architect—
etching intention into
every choice,
every stillness,
every brave leap toward meaning.

To be the architect of your legacy is to know:
every decision lays a brick,
every value becomes a beam.

Each act of courage strengthens the frame
on which your future—and perhaps others'—
will rise.

Purpose is not born in reflection alone.
It demands embodiment.

As Goethe, in his Italian journey, wrote:
"Knowing is not enough; we must apply.
Willing is not enough; we must do."

And so,
we must.

Vitruvius taught that great architecture must hold:
Firmitas, *Utilitas*, and *Venustas*—
Strength, Function, and Beauty.

So too must our lives.

Let our foundation be firm—
rooted in principles that
endure beyond circumstance.

Let our purpose be of use—
not only serving ourselves,
but lifting others as it rises.

And let our form carry beauty—
not the polished kind that fades,
but the quiet grace that comes
from coherence,
from alignment,
from truth made visible.

Nothing of worth is built in haste.
No lasting structure rises without change.

Frank Lloyd Wright's believed in
organic architecture:
form must arise in harmony
with its environment.

So too must purpose unfold—
not forced,
but discovered.
Not imposed,
but nurtured—
in balance with both inner compass
and the outer world.

To live with purpose is to listen—
to your potential,
to your surroundings,
and to the needs beyond yourself.

Progress is not a privilege for the few.
It is a structure we raise together.
We build not only for the present,
but for those unseen,
unborn,
unheard.

John Rawls's vision of *justice*
lies not only in personal success,
but in shaping a world
where fairness is felt,
and dignity is shared.

Purpose is not a solitary pursuit.
It is a sacred offering—
where the self and the collective
move in harmony.

A purposeful life does not ask only:
What will I build?
But also:
Why will it matter?

It is not crafted merely to function,
but to elevate.
Not only to endure,
but to illuminate.

Marcus Aurelius wrote:
"What we do now echoes in eternity."

And so, purpose imbues
each action with permanence—
not through possession,
but through impact.

Your life is not a scattering of events.
It is an intentional rising—
a creation woven
in trust,
in truth,
in tenderness.

Not in the loudness of achievement,
but in the quiet scaffolding of
integrity,
humility,
and love.

Long after the titles are forgotten,
long after the applause fades,
what remains is the soul of your work—
the unseen, yet indelible foundation
you chose to build:
your legacy.

This is how we create lives that last,
not only for ourselves,
but for the world
we briefly touch
and permanently influence.

May those who walk in our footsteps
feel not only our presence,
but our purpose—
and in that remembrance,
awaken their own.

Letter 22: Dear Manifestor

MAPPING THE VIBRATING FIELDS OF INFINITE POTENTIAL

The future is not ahead of you; it is all around you, right now, existing as overlapping probability fields where each vision you hold, each emotion you sustain, strengthens one potential while weakening others.

Reality is not fixed,
It hums—
vibrating with infinite potentials,
a living field of unseen possibilities.

What appears solid
is merely energy,
briefly slowed into form,
then dissolving again
into the boundless.

Matter is a pause
in the stream of formlessness.
A crystallized vibration,
only to return
into the boundless field from
which it came.

You are not simply an observer.
You are a co-creator,
a participant in the unfolding
of what becomes real.

Beneath the surface of
apparent solidity lies
a shimmering ocean of possibility—
a quantum field where all potentials
exist simultaneously,
overlapping,
resonating,
waiting.

Not for time to pass,
but for your awareness to choose,
for your intention to summon
form from the formless.

You were taught to
navigate a world already built—
a landscape of fixed facts,
and steady laws.

But this, too, is an illusion—
a habit of perception,
not a law of existence.

Quantum physics has shattered that illusion:
you are not separate from what you see.
You are entangled with it.

As John Wheeler proposed,
we live in a *participatory universe*,
not a mechanical system,
but a conscious unfolding
where the act of observing
becomes an act of creation.

Consciousness is not
an afterthought of matter.
It is the stillness
from which form arises,
the current that gives matter its movement.

David Bohm named this the *implicate order*:
the hidden wholeness beneath appearance,
the ground from which
all things come into being.

The world you know,
the explicate order,
is a ripple—
temporary, visible,
but born from the unseen.

You do not walk through a fixed reality.
You engage with it—
shaping it
with your frequency,
your focus,
your belief.

The future is not ahead of you.
It is all around you,
existing as overlapping fields of possibility
each one waiting for your resonance.

Every vision you hold,
each emotion you sustain,
strengthens one potential
while dissolving another.

To set an intention,
is not to wish.
It is to align.

You begin to vibrate
in resonance with a certain possibility
and in doing so,
the invisible becomes probable.

Heisenberg's *uncertainty principle* reminds us:
the more precisely you know
a particle's position,
the less you can know
its momentum—and vice versa.

And so it is
with your own becoming.

The more firmly you cling
to the *"how,"*
the more you narrow
the vastness of *"what could be."*

True manifestation is not control.
It is attunement.
It is the sacred balance:
focused clarity
paired with radical openness.

As Rupert Sheldrake's *morphic resonance* suggests:
your thoughts,
your inner states,
do not vanish into silence.
They ripple outward,
joining fields of memory and intention
shared across time and space.

To align with your dream
is to amplify
what already exists in potential—
to call it into coherence
through presence and belief.

So ask not,
"How do I force this into form?"
but rather,
"What field am I tuning into?
What reality is my being energizing?"

If you believe,
"If I cannot see the path, it must not exist,"
remember:
the path does not precede your steps.
It follows in response to them.

You are not reacting to life.
You are in an eternal dialogue
with the intelligence that
flows through all.

Your deepest purpose is not something to find.
It is a resonance you come to recognize.

It does not arrive with instruction.
It reveals itself through
intuition,
sensation,
the subtle pull
of what feels aligned.

And when you trust that pull,
you enter the quantum flow—
where life feels less like effort,
and more like emergence.

Where creation is not born of force,
but of surrender.

Where manifestation arises
not from scarcity,
but from alignment
to a field already holding
what belongs to you.

Hold your vision lightly
but faithfully,
not as a fixed outcome,
but as a living frequency.

Remember:
delay is not denial,
it is recalibration—
a reweaving of elements
until your readiness
meets the reality you seek.

Timing is not mechanical,
it is energetic—
an alignment between your inner state
and the reality you are calling in.

And so,
be present.
Now is the only access point to the infinite.

Be intentional.
Your focus is shaping what becomes.

Be in communion,
not with certainty,
but with the intelligence
that flows through all things.

And in that communion,
create not from fear,
but from surrendered alignment.

Letter 23: Dear Eternal Becoming

THE JOURNEY BEYOND ARRIVAL

There is no arrival, no singular moment of completeness because your horizon moves as you move, expanding with every step.

Arrival is but a breath
between movements—
a fleeting pause
between what has been
and what longs to be.

Beyond every arrival,
another horizon always beckons.

We are often taught to believe that
fulfillment, clarity, and success
await at some distant summit—
that if we reach *there*,
we will finally *arrive.*

But as soon as we touch what once felt distant,
the horizon recedes—
subtly yet inexorably.

Our longing stretches further,
our vision widens,
and once more,
life reveals again:
there is more.

For the horizon moves as you move,
responding to your becoming.

What once felt like an ending
reveals itself as a beginning in disguise—
a passage into a deeper becoming,
a more luminous version of you
stepping forward from the shadow
of who you were.

Nietzsche's *Übermensch*
is not one who arrives,
but one who transcends—
rising beyond former selves,
refusing to settle into definition.

The *Übermensch* becomes—
ceaselessly evolving,
relentlessly reshaping
through will, challenge, and vision.

To live fully is
to release the illusion of finality.
To recognize that growth is not a destination,
but a way of being.

In the spirit of *wabi-sabi,*
beauty is found not in flawlessness,
but in the gentle wear of existence—
the cracks that reveal history,
the asymmetries that hold character,
the unfinished edges that
speak of growth still in motion.

Like *anicca,*
the Buddhist truth of impermanence,
your becoming
is not a singular event,
but an ongoing transformation.

Nothing is permanent—
not the self,
not the world,
not even the thoughts
we hold from one moment
to the next.

And in Nietzsche's
notion of becoming (*Werden*),
identity is not a fixed state,
but a fluid expression.
The self of yesterday
has already softened into memory.
The self of today
is already dissolving into tomorrow.

The body ages.
The mind rewires itself.
Emotion ebbs and flows.
Reality itself is never still.

To cling to the past
is to resist the essence of what is—
for all existence flows,
and in that flow,
becomes.

To live is to surrender to this unfolding,
to trust that no version of you
is final.

There is no singular arrival,
no ultimate revelation
that silences all doubt.

There is only deeper seeing
and fuller becoming.

For every answer births new questions.
And that, too, is wisdom—
to know more,
and in that knowing,
to humbly realize
how much remains veiled.

You were never meant to remain.
You were meant to evolve—
to expand beyond every line
that once defined you.

As José Ortega y Gasset wrote:
"Life is a series of collisions with the future;
it is not the sum of what we have been
but what we yearn to be."

To become is to greet those collisions
not with resistance,
but with curiosity—
to let the future shape you
as much as you shape it.

Evolution is not rejection of the past,
but its expansion—
a devotion to movement
over arrival,
transformation over stability,
wonder over finality.

You are not here to arrive.
You are here to unfold—
gracefully,
imperfectly,
and endlessly.

And in that unfolding,
there is beauty,
there is brilliance in motion.

Honor your becoming.
Honor the threshold you now stand upon.
Honor the beauty
of this moment in-between—
no longer who you were,
not yet who you will be,
but gloriously
and courageously
becoming beyond arrival.

Letter 24: Dear Guardian of the Flame

TENDING THE FIRE OF PURPOSE

Your flame does not burn in isolation; it is not separate from the fire of your ancestors, nor from the light that will illuminate your descendants.

Within you burns a sacred flame—
your deepest purpose,
your most authentic truth,
your vision for what could be—
and yet,
it was never yours alone.

It was kindled long before your birth,
passed through generations of hands,
tended by innumerable hearts,
protected through centuries of
darkness and light.

You are neither its creator,
nor its final keeper.
You are its momentary guardian,
entrusted with its tending
for the brief flicker of your existence.

The light that illuminates your life
does not begin with you,
nor will it end.

It flows through you,
transformed by your care,
but never fully contained.

Heidegger understood this when he spoke of *Dasein*:
our existence not as isolated beings,
but as manifestations of
a continuous becoming through time.

You do not exist merely in the present.
You embody the convergence
of past and future,
standing as living bridge between
what has been
and what will be.

The flame you tend
is not separate from the fires
your ancestors carried.
It is not apart from the light
your descendants
will one day protect.

It is one continuous burning—
a sacred thread of awareness
connecting generations
in an unbroken thread.

Even your body is an archive.
Epigenetics reveals
that the stories your ancestors lived
did not vanish.
They live in your cells.

The trauma your grandmother could not heal,
the resilience your grandfather
developed through hardship,
the choices your ancestors made for survival—
they are not just stories.

They are biological imprints,
written in the structure of your being,
influencing how your
own genes express themselves.

When you heal,
you do not heal alone.
You purify what was carried,
fortify what was weakened,
and refine the flame that will be passed on.

Jung understood this
greater field of consciousness—
a collective psyche,
a vast interior space
through which we are all connected.

In transforming your awareness,
you reshape the architecture
of this shared inheritance.

The flame you carry
holds both
radiance and shadow—
gifts and burdens,
truth and distortion.

To be its keeper
is to practice sacred discernment:
to protect what gives life,
and transform what once brought pain.

To tend this fire with awareness
is to partake in a sacred tradition:
to maintain coherence across generations,
ensuring that what matters most
is not lost in the noise of change.

You stand at a precipice in history.
The pace of the world threatens
the continuity of consciousness itself.

Many flames have been forgotten.
Many have been extinguished.

And so,
your stewardship has never been more vital.

Ask yourself:
What wisdom has been entrusted to me?
What part of this fire calls for protection?
What must I transform before it is passed on?
What light am I uniquely here to add?

This is not a call
to preserve the past in amber,
but to honor what endures
while allowing a new iteration of truth.

It is not resistance to change,
but reverence within it.
It is conscious stewardship,
offering your hands
not to hold the flame still,
but to guide its brightness.

In quiet moments,
when the noise dims,
you may feel them—
the long line of tenders
who came before you,
and those yet to come.

Your life is not a solitary journey.
It is part of a much vaster unfolding.

To recognize this
is to awaken to
the sacred responsibility
entrusted to your care.

For in tending this flame with love,
you participate in a continuity
far greater than yourself—
the living fire of consciousness,
moving through time,
illuminating the path ahead.

You are both heir and ancestor,
keeper and creator.

This is your legacy.

And when this chapter of tending ends,
may the fire burn—
brighter,
clearer,
stronger—
than when it reached your hands.

And so,
tend it:
with wisdom.
with gratitude,
with awareness,
with reverence.

Not only for yourself,
but for all who came before you,
and all who are still to come.

EPILOGUE

THE JOURNEY THROUGH THE 24 LETTERS

As you journeyed through the *24 letters*,
you encountered living archetypes—
each one awakening your full potential.

Each one,
a facet of your becoming,
a voice calling you toward the convergence of
purpose,
alignment,
and transformation.

It began with the *visionary*—
the one who answered the call to rise,
reaching beyond what is,
into what longs to be.

Then came the *sovereign mind*,
revealing that thought,
when mastered,
is not only the seed of creation,
but the architect
of experience, of self, of civilization.

With that foundation,
you met the *alchemist*—
who taught you the sacred transmutation:
that pain, when honored, becomes wisdom;
and fire, when faced, becomes the forge.

From that fire rose the *warrior of will*—
quietly resilient,
defiant of impulse,
disciplined in pursuit of
what truly matters.

Beside the *warrior of will* stood the *keeper of energy,*
reminding you that attention is defining—
not in declarations,
but in the unseen choices
that define your becoming.

From empowerment, you stepped into transformation.

The *stillness seeker* offered you a paradox:
stillness is not absence of action,
but presence refined—
the clarity from which
all intentional movement begins.

Then the *growth seeker* reframed evolution—
not as accumulation,
but as unfolding:
a spiraling dialogue
between where you stand
and what you are becoming.

But transformation demands courage.

And so arrived the *sailor of the unknown*,
revealing that uncertainty is not emptiness,
but fertile ground for possibility—
where vision roots before it blooms.

From that ground rose the *phoenix*,
proving that we rise not despite the fire,
but because of it.
Rebirth is not a return,
but a purification of
everything you have endured.

The *keeper of time* liberated you
from the tyranny of more,
reminding you that fulfillment
is not a distant destination—
it lives here,
in the presence you allow now.

With time redefined, you encountered
the *keeper of balance—*
who revealed that opposites
do not compete,
they complete.
Each polarity births its counterpart,
and in their tension,
wholeness forms.

With this equilibrium,
you entered alignment—
into a life attuned
to your deepest truths.

At the heart of this alignment stood the *trustor*,
offering the wisdom that self-trust
is not blind optimism,
but brave allegiance
to your inner knowing.

From trust, the *keeper of integrity* emerged
as the lived harmony
between inner truth and outer action.

Then the *authentic self* reminded you:
authenticity is not indulgence—
it is courageous honesty,
standing unarmored
in the fullness of your truth.

The *lover of the self* declared:
self-compassion is the foundation
from which all other love flows.

The *lover of life* dared you
to fall in love with the world once more—
not to conquer or control,
but to engage with reverence,
as both witness and co-creator.

In that reverence,
the *artist of gratitude* appeared—
showing that gratitude is not a feeling,
but a way of seeing,
turning the ordinary into sacred.

Turning inward and outward,
the *mirror gazer* presented
relationships as reflections—
each one a mirror,
each one a message.

From alignment, you turned toward vision and purpose.

The *dreamer of greatness* proclaimed:
vision is not fantasy,
but a refusal to accept
that what is
must define what will be.

To turn vision to impact,
the *pioneer* invited you
to question the frameworks themselves—
not merely to navigate them,
but to reimagine them.

Yet vision demands structure.

The *architect of legacy* showed you:
purpose is not stumbled upon,
but built—
choice by choice,
value by value.

Then came the *manifestor*,
pulling back the veil:
reality is not fixed—
it is resonant,
responsive, and alive.

The *eternal becoming* released you
from the illusion of arrival—
you are always evolving:
learning, unlearning, transforming—
becoming who you need to be now,
before growing into
who you are meant to become next.

And finally,
the *guardian of the flame* stepped forth,
placing in your hands
a light only you can tend—
a torch passed through generations,
illuminating what's possible
for all who follow.

These archetypes were never symbols to admire.
They were activations—
energies awakening within you,
each one a prism of your infinite potential.

And now,
you stand at the edge of creation.
No longer who you were.
Not yet all you will become.

The questions that remain cannot be answered for you.
They must be lived.

What fires will you tend?
What boundaries will you transcend?
What visions will you dare into form?
What hidden parts of you will finally emerge?

The world does not need your perfection.
It needs your presence.
Not your achievements,
but your alignment.
Not your certainty,
but your courage.

Let your presence declare:
another way is possible.
Let your actions reveal:
consciousness can forge reality.
Let your becoming testify:
intention and integrity birth new realms.

You live at the nexus of infinite potential—
where past and future meet,
where the personal touches the collective,
where limitation dissolves into light.

Do not dim your light to make others comfortable.
Do not shrink your vision to fit the familiar.
Do not silence your truth to preserve false peace.

You were made for more.
You were made to create.
Not through grand spectacle,
but through conscious choice,
aligned action,
and enduring purpose.

The fire is yours to tend.
The edge is yours to cross.
The future is yours to design.

Rise.
Not because the journey is gentle,
but because the rising itself
is an act of reverence—
a devotion,
a declaration
that your becoming
is nothing less than sacred.

And when you rise,
may life gift you
moments of unexpected beauty.
May you receive them
with the quiet knowng that
you deserve every one of them.

THE 24 ARCHETYPES

1. The Visionary
2. The Sovereign Mind
3. The Alchemist
4. The Warrior Of Will
5. The Keeper Of Energy
6. The Stillness Seeker
7. The Growth Seeker
8. The Sailor Of The Unknown
9. The Phoenix
10. The Keeper Of Time
11. The Keeper Of Balance
12. The Trustor
13. The Keeper Of Integrity
14. The Authentic Self
15. The Lover Of The Self
16. The Lover Of Life
17. The Artist Of Gratitude
18. The Mirror Gazer
19. The Dreamer Of Greatness
20. The Pioneer
21. The Architect Of Legacy
22. The Manifestor
23. The Eternal Becoming
24. The Guardian Of The Flame

NOTES

Active Information Bohm's concept proposing that consciousness itself influences potential outcomes in the universe. Consciousness is not a passive observer of reality but rather plays a role in the process of its unfolding. (Bohm, D. (1980). *Wholeness and the implicate order.* Routledge & Kegan Paul.)

Aesthetic Freedom Schiller's concept where creativity harmonizes instinct and reason, liberating the self from both impulse and rigidity. (Schiller, F. (1967). *On the Aesthetic Education of Man.* Oxford University Press.)

Akrasia Aristotle's concept of "weakness of will." Living virtuously requires not just knowledge of what is right but the discipline to act accordingly. (Aristotle. (1999). *Nicomachean Ethics* (T. Irwin, Trans.). Hackett Publishing Company. Original work published ca. 350 BCE.)

Allegory of the Cave Plato's allegory about those who turn toward the light, daring to see what others do not. Yet to see more is to be burdened by more—to know truths that unsettle, to envision futures that do not yet exist. (Plato. (1974). *The Republic* (G. M. A. Grube, Trans.). Hackett Publishing Company. Original work published ca. 380 BCE.)

Amor Fati Nietzsche's philosophical concept meaning "love of fate." The radical embrace of all that befalls you, finding beauty and necessity in all experiences. The most radical gratitude is loving fate itself, embracing adversity as a necessary condition for growth and appreciation. (Nietzsche, F. (1974). *The Gay Science* (W. Kaufmann, Trans.). Vintage Books. Original work published 1882.)

Anicca Buddhist concept of impermanence. The understanding that nothing is permanent—not the self, not the world, not even the thoughts we hold from one moment to the next.

Antifragility Taleb's concept describing systems that gain strength from volatility. The sovereign mind does not break under pressure; it extracts wisdom from volatility. Those who scatter their energy become fragile, exhausted, lost. Those who harness it become unshakable, thriving through disruption. (Taleb, N. N. (2012). *Antifragile: Things That Gain from Disorder*. Random House.)

Apatheia Stoic concept meaning freedom from disturbing passions through rational self-discipline, not apathy, but inner equanimity. (Epictetus. (1995). *The Discourses* (R. Hard, Trans.). Everyman. Original work published ca. 108 CE)

Apeiron Anaximander's concept of "the Boundless, the Inexhaustible"—describing reality as an infinite, ever-generating source, from where all things come into being, dissolve, and return. Anaximander. (Cited in secondary sources, ca. 610-546 BCE)

Arigatai Japanese concept teaching that gratitude encompasses all that life offers—including difficulty, impermanence, and undercurrents. It does not separate joy from hardship, gain from loss, but acknowledges both as life's necessary facets.

Aufhebung Hegel's dialectical process where contradictions are transcended and preserved in a higher synthesis. Aufhebung means to lift, cancel, and preserve—capturing the paradox of transformation where nothing is lost, but everything is reimagined. (Hegel, G. W. F. (1977). *Phenomenology of Spirit* (A. V. Miller, Trans.). Oxford University Press. Original work published 1807)

Autarkeia Represents the Cynic and, later, the Stoic ideal of self-sufficiency as the true form of freedom and excellence. (Epictetus. (1995). *The Discourses* (R. Hard, Trans.). Everyman. Original work published ca. 108 CE)

Being and Time Heidegger's concept reminding us that existence is not passive. We do not simply exist; we actively engage with the world through choice, action, and intention. Also includes his notion of temporality: "Temporality temporalizes as a future which makes present in the process of having been." (Heidegger, M. (1962). *Being and Time* (J. Macquarrie & E. Robinson, Trans.). Harper & Row. Original work published 1927)

Butterfly Effect From chaos theory, revealing that transition is not evidence of breakdown but breakthrough—systems reorganizing toward greater complexity.

Categorical Imperative Kant's ethical framework asking: "Could I will my action to become universal law?" Living this imperative means creating a world where, if all followed suit, justice would naturally flourish. (Kant, I. (1993). *Grounding for the Metaphysics of Morals* (J. W. Ellington, Trans.). Hackett Publishing Company. Original work published 1785)

Collective Unconscious Jung's concept revealing that we are not isolated in our thinking. We are connected to a shared pool of human experience, archetypes, and symbols—patterns that transcend individual lives. When you work to transform your awareness, you simultaneously reshape this shared architecture—contributing to the evolution of humanity's collective psyche. (Jung, C. G. (1968). *The Archetypes and the Collective Unconscious* (R. F. C. Hull, Trans.). Princeton University Press. Original work published 1934)

Cognitive Reframing Psychological technique teaching us that our interpretation of events determines our response. The alchemist does not ask, "Why did this happen to me?" but rather, "What can I create from this?" By changing how we view an event, we transform not just our perspective but our actual experience and outcomes. (Beck, A. T. (1979). *Cognitive Therapy and the Emotional Disorders.* International Universities Press.)

Cogito, ergo sum Descartes' declaration: "I think, therefore I am." This extends beyond mere existence to mean that thought is the foundation of reality itself. (Descartes, R. (1984). *Meditations on First Philosophy* (J. Cottingham, Trans.). Cambridge University Press. Original work published 1641)

Counter-conduct Foucault's concept of deliberate rebellion against subtle systems of control. Resisting pulls on your energy requires a deliberate rebellion against subtle systems of control. (Foucault, M. (2007). *Security, Territory, Population: Lectures at the Collège de France, 1977-1978* (G. Burchell, Trans.). Palgrave Macmillan.)

Dasein Heidegger's concept of our existence not as isolated beings but as manifestations of a continuous unfolding through time. You do not exist merely in the present. You embody the convergence of past and future, standing as living bridge between what has been and what will be. (Heidegger, M. (1962). *Being and Time* (J. Macquarrie & E. Robinson, Trans.). Harper & Row. Original work published 1927)

Default Mode Network Brain system triggered during stillness— responsible for creativity, insight, and profound reflection. In these moments of silence, the mind regenerates, processes complexity, and reaches profound insight.

Dialectic Hegel's teaching that growth occurs through the synthesis of opposites—thesis and antithesis merging into a higher understanding (synthesis). Our minds evolve not by avoiding contradiction, but by engaging with it. (Hegel, G. W. F. (1977). *Phenomenology of Spirit* (A. V. Miller, Trans.). Oxford University Press. Original work published 1807)

Differentiation Psychological capacity to weigh external advice without being dominated by it. Trusting yourself is not a rejection of external input but a form of differentiation—the ability to consider others' perspectives while maintaining your own center. Highly differentiated individuals can stand firm in their values even when those around them disagree, maintaining connection without sacrificing authenticity. (Bowen, M. (1978). *Family Therapy in Clinical Practice.* Jason Aronson.)

Diffusion Curve Rogers' sociological concept describing how innovation spreads—beginning with a small percentage of early adopters before reaching wider acceptance. (Rogers, E. M. (1962). *Diffusion of Innovations.* Free Press.)

Dissipative Structures Theory Prigogine's theory revealing that systems do not evolve through stability. They evolve through disruption, through being pushed beyond equilibrium. In such non-equilibrium conditions, systems can spontaneously self-organize into new, more complex structures. When a system reaches a critical threshold, it will either break down into chaos or reorganize into something stronger, more adaptive, more complete. (Prigogine, I. (1977). *Self-Organization in Non-Equilibrium Systems.* Wiley.)

Divine Comedy Dante Alighieri's work written not as a lament, but as an odyssey through suffering toward transcendence during his exile from his homeland. (Alighieri, D. (1995). *The Divine Comedy* (A. Mandelbaum, Trans.). Everyman's Library. Original work published ca. 1320)

Divine Milieu Teilhard de Chardin's concept of a force not just in motion, but propelling existence toward complexity, evolution, and higher being. (Teilhard de Chardin, P. (1959). *The Phenomenon of Man* (B. Wall, Trans.). Harper & Row. Original work published 1955)

Dunning-Kruger Effect Psychological finding that true growth begins with humility. It requires the ability to recognize what you do not yet know and having the courage to confront it. (Dunning, D., & Kruger, J. (1999). *Unskilled And Unaware of It: How Difficulties In Recognizing One's Own Incompetence Lead To Inflated Self-Assessments*. Journal of Personality and Social Psychology, 77(6), 1121-1134.)

Duration (Durée) Bergson's concept revealing that time is not a measurable, linear sequence, but rather a qualitative, conscious experience. The more present we are, the more time expands. (Bergson, H. (1910). *Time and Free Will: An Essay on The Immediate Data Of Consciousness* (F. L. Pogson, Trans.). George Allen & Unwin. Original work published 1889)

Élan Vital Bergson's concept of the raw, creative impulse of life, reminding us that energy is not just for survival. It is for transformation, for expansion, for becoming. (Bergson, H. (1998). *Creative evolution* (A. Mitchell, Trans.). Dover Publications. Original work published 1907)

Enantiodromia Ancient Greek principle that everything eventually transforms into its opposite. The height of order gives birth to chaos. The depth of darkness summons light.

Epigenetics Scientific field showing how our cells carry the encoded experiences of those who came before us. The trauma your grandmother could not heal, the resilience your grandfather developed through hardship—these are not merely stories but biological imprints.

Erlebnis Husserl's concept of "lived experience," arguing that the passage of time is not a string of discrete points but a continuous flow, where past, present, and future converge in consciousness. (Husserl, E. (1991). *On The Phenomenology of The Consciousness of Internal Time* (J. B. Brough, Trans.). Kluwer Academic Publishers. Original work published 1928)

Ethics of Ambiguity Simone de Beauvoir's recognition that human life at its root is ambiguous—we are at once free yet constrained, isolated yet connected, finite yet reaching for infinity. (de Beauvoir, S. (1948). *The Ethics of Ambiguity* (B. Frechtman, Trans.). Philosophical Library. Original work published 1947)

Existential Authenticity Philosophical concept underpinning the journey to authentic selfhood. To be authentic is not to wear a mask, but to stand, unarmored, in the truth of who you are. It is the refusal to be a construct of expectation, the reclamation of your own becoming—shedding social conditioning to allow your essential nature to emerge through conscious choice. (Sartre, J.-P. (1956). *Being And Nothingness* (H. E. Barnes, Trans.). Philosophical Library. Original work published 1943)

Eudaimonia Aristotle's concept of flourishing that endures through every season, not fleeting pleasure that comes and goes.(Aristotle. (1999). *Nicomachean Ethics* (T. Irwin, Trans.). Hackett Publishing Company. Original work published ca. 350 BCE)

Experience-Dependent Neuroplasticity Neurological concept showing that what you repeatedly focus on strengthens through neural rewiring. Your brain rewires itself to prioritize the thoughts you entertain most frequently.

Felt Sense Eugene Gendlin's term for the holistic bodily awareness that holds implicit knowing, not yet verbalized. When you listen to your internal guidance, you are tuning into bodily sensations that signal meaning before cognitive understanding forms. This pre-conceptual understanding your body has before your mind forms words around it is fundamental to authentic decision-making and self-trust. (Gendlin, E. T. (1978). *Focusing*. Everest House.)

Firmitas, Utilitas, Venustas Vitruvius' architectural principles of Strength, Function, and Beauty applied to a life's foundation and purpose. All structures must embody these three qualities. (Vitruvius. (1960). *The Ten Books on Architecture* (M. H. Morgan, Trans.). Dover Publications. Original work published ca. 15 BCE)

First Law of Thermodynamics Physical principle revealing that energy cannot be created or destroyed, only transformed. What feels like irrevocable loss is energy changing forms.

Flow Csikszentmihalyi's concept of peak performance as not a product of stress or sheer effort, but of deep alignment—where challenge meets skill, and self-consciousness dissolves into pure engagement. To live in Csikszentmihalyi's flow is to embody both stillness and motion, presence and purpose, awareness and action. (Csikszentmihalyi, M. (1990). *Flow: The Psychology of Optimal Experience.* Harper & Row.)

Gelassenheit Heidegger's philosophical attitude of "releasement" or "letting-be" as an alternative to our obsessive desire for control. (Heidegger, M. (1966). *Discourse On Thinking* (J. M. Anderson & E. H. Freund, Trans.). Harper & Row. Original work published 1959)

Hedonic Treadmill Effect Psychological pattern where satisfaction fades regardless of achievement, creating a cycle of deferred arrival.

Historicity Gadamer's notion that our future cannot be separate from our present and past. Your thoughts are not born in a vacuum; they are reflections of the traditions, ideas, and experiences that precede you. (Gadamer, H.-G. (2004). *Truth And Method* (J. Weinsheimer & D. G. Marshall, Trans.). Continuum. Original work published 1960)

I-It and I-Thou Buber's distinction between two ways to relate. In an I-It relationship, we see the other as a role, a function, a means to an end. In an I-Thou relationship, we meet them as they are—not as a projection of our desires. (Buber, M. (1958). *I And Thou* (R. G. Smith, Trans.). Charles Scribner's Sons. Original work published 1923)

Implicate Order Bohm's concept of a hidden dimension of infinite potential from which all things arise. The physical world (the explicate order) is a ripple—temporary, visible, but born from the unseen. (Bohm, D. (1980). *Wholeness and the Implicate Order*. Routledge & Kegan Paul.)

Interbeing Thich Nhat Hanh's based on Mahayana Buddhist principles taught that we do not exist in isolation. Just as the moon does not shine without the sun, we do not fully see ourselves without the presence of others. (Thich Nhat Hanh. (1987). *Interbeing: Fourteen Guidelines for Engaged Buddhism.* Parallax Press.)

Internal Time-Consciousness Husserl's concept that the passage of time is not a string of discrete points but a continuous flow, where past, present, and future converge in consciousness. (Husserl, E. (1991). *On The Phenomenology of The Consciousness of Internal Time* (J. B. Brough, Trans.). Kluwer Academic Publishers. Original work published 1928)

Involuntary poetizing (unwillkührliches Dichten) Kant's concept describing the dream state where imagination spontaneously generates images and narratives without conscious control. During sleep, the mind engages in this unintentional creative production where dream images appear "as if external," and mental fictions that were faint during waking hours gain "such force, clarity, and distinction" that they rival the truths of waking life. (Kant, I. (1798). *Anthropology from a Pragmatic Point of View*. Cambridge University Press.)

Interoception The ability to perceive your internal states accurately. Learning to access inner guidance is about developing interoception—the foundation for emotional awareness, decision-making, and self-trust. Research suggests that stronger interoceptive abilities correlate with better emotional regulation and sense of self. (Craig, A. D. (2003). *Interoception: The Sense of The Physiological Condition of The Body*. Current Opinion in Neurobiology, 13(4), 500-505.)

Intrinsic Motivation Deci and Ryan transformed motivation theory by challenging behaviorist models. Instead of viewing humans as simply responding to rewards and punishments, they revealed our innate tendencies toward growth and well-being that flourish or diminish depending on our social environment. (Deci, E. L., & Ryan, R. M. (1985). *Intrinsic Motivation and Self-Determination in Human Behavior*. Plenum Press.)

Italian Journey Goethe's work reminding us that "Knowing is not enough; we must apply. Willing is not enough; we must do." Purpose demands action, not just contemplation. (Goethe, J. W. (1982). *Italian journey* (W. H. Auden & E. Mayer, Trans.). Penguin Books. Original work published 1816-1817)

Kampf um Anerkennung Hegel's concept of the "fight for recognition." Selfhood is not born in isolation; it is shaped in the space where we are truly seen. But that recognition must be earned not by conformity, but by the bold assertion of truth. (Hegel, G. W. F. (1977). *Phenomenology of Spirit* (A. V. Miller, Trans.). Oxford University Press. Original work published 1807)

Kalon Plato's concept of beauty that transcends appearance to embody the soul's perfection through virtue. This higher beauty emerges not despite our struggles but through them, as we align our inner nature with truth. (Plato. (1997). *Complete Works* (J. M. Cooper & D. S. Hutchinson, Eds.). Hackett Publishing Company.)

Karuna Buddhist concept of compassion forming the bedrock of mindfulness and empathy, guiding us to nurture ourselves with the same care we offer to others.

Kintsugi Japanese art of repairing broken pottery with gold, teaching that brokenness is not meant to be hidden, it is meant to be honored. Cracks are filled with gold, turning fractures into art.

Last Human Freedom Viktor Frankl's concept of the ability to choose one's response, to assign meaning to suffering, and through that meaning, to transcend it. Your mind will follow the meaning you give it. (Frankl, V. E. (1959). *Man's Search for Meaning.* Beacon Press.)

Law of Serendipity The principle that the most profound transformations often emerge from the unexpected. Growth, insight, and discovery arise from navigating ambiguity with curiosity rather than fear.

Leap of Faith Kierkegaard's concept of the courageous commitment to trust in something not yet fully seen or proven. (Kierkegaard, S. (1985). *Fear and Trembling* (A. Hannay, Trans.). Penguin Books. Original work published 1843)

Lila Tagore's concept of divine play—an endless unfolding of creation and dissolution, where every moment is a divine invitation to participate with wonder, with creativity, with surrender. (Tagore, R. (1913). *Gitanjali: Song Offerings* (W. B. Yeats, Intro.). Macmillan.)

Liminality The experience of the in-between of what was and what will be—evokes unease, yet it is within this threshold that our most profound transformations take place. In transition, we are unmade and remade, shaped by the unknown into what we are becoming.

Liquid Modernity Bauman's concept of a world where social structures no longer solidify but remain in constant flux. Previous generations could build lives around stable institutions, but today's reality is characterized by fluidity and continuous change. (Bauman, Z. (2000). *Liquid Modernity*. Polity Press.)

Mauvaise Foi Sartre's concept of "bad faith"—the self-deception of surrendering your freedom to the safety of an imposed identity, the false comfort of belonging at the cost of being. (Sartre, J.-P. (1956). *Being And Nothingness* (H. E. Barnes, Trans.). Philosophical Library. Original work published 1943)

Marshmallow Experiment Landmark psychological study showing that children who delayed gratification outperformed their peers in nearly every measure of success decades later. (Mischel, W. (2014). *The Marshmallow Test: Mastering Self-Control*. Little, Brown and Company.)

Metta Buddhist concept of loving-kindness forming the bedrock of mindfulness and empathy, guiding us to nurture ourselves with the same care we offer to others.

Mindfulness The practice of maintaining awareness of the present moment without judgment. Creating space between stimulus and response—where you can feel what's true beneath the noise. This practice facilitates many of the states described in the letters, including stillness, authenticity, presence, and self-trust. (Kabat-Zinn, J. (1994). *Wherever You Go, There You Are: Mindfulness Meditation In Everyday Life*. Hyperion.)

Mono no Aware Japanese aesthetic concept recognizing that beauty and impermanence are one. The cherry blossom is precious not despite its fall, but because of it.

Mushin Japanese Zen concept of "no-mind"—suggesting that true mastery begins where thought falls silent, when knowing dissolves into effortless, intuitive wisdom. This state is especially important in martial arts, where practitioners aim to act without calculation or conscious thought—responding naturally with perfect clarity. (Suzuki, D. T. (1959). *Zen And Japanese Culture.* Princeton University Press.)

Morphic Resonance Sheldrake's theory that patterns of consciousness extend beyond individuals—fields of memory and intention shared across time and space. (Sheldrake, R. (1981). *A New Science of Life: The Hypothesis of Formative Causation.* J.P. Tarcher.)

Nietzschean Dream Theory (Schein) Nietzsche's concept of dreams as an expression of the Apollonian impulse, where the self creates a "measured world of beauty" through Schein (semblance or illusion). This illusion overlays the Dionysian chaos beneath consciousness, temporarily redeeming existence through aesthetic appearances. The dream state represents the human capacity to transform chaotic reality into ordered, beautiful images. (Nietzsche, F. (1967). *The Birth of Tragedy* (W. Kaufmann, Trans.). Random House. Original work published 1872.)

Natality Hannah Arendt's concept of the radical capacity to initiate, disrupt, and shape the world through new beginnings. To pioneer is to embody this act of creation. (Arendt, H. (1958). *The Human Condition.* University of Chicago Press.)

Nous Plato's concept of higher intellect that discerns truth beyond appearances. The sovereign mind does not consume information. It filters, defines, and redefines its own understanding. (Plato. (1997). *Complete Works* (J. M. Cooper & D. S. Hutchinson, Eds.). Hackett Publishing Company.)

Officium Cicero's concept of the duty one owes to oneself as much as to society. Integrity reveals itself most purely when no eyes are watching, when no praise will follow, when only you will know the choice you made. (Cicero. (1991). *On Duties* (M. T. Griffin & E. M. Atkins, Trans.). Cambridge University Press. Original work published 44 BCE)

Oneness Spinoza's concept that your energy is not separate from the universe. It moves through you, shapes you, ripples into everything. When you align with this truth, you stop fighting against the flow of life and start moving with it. (Spinoza, B. (1992). *Ethics* (S. Shirley, Trans.). Hackett Publishing Company. Original work published 1677)

Openness to Experience Costa and McCrae's personality trait most related to cognitive flexibility and creativity. A mind that resists change becomes rigid; a mind that adapts evolves and thrives. (Costa, P. T., & McCrae, R. R. (1992). *Revised NEO Personality Inventory (NEO-PI-R) And NEO Five-Factor Inventory (NEO-FFI) Professional Manual.* Psychological Assessment Resources.)

Organic Architecture Frank Lloyd Wright's concept that true creation comes not from force, but from discovery—growing in harmony with its environment, shaped by both vision and context. (Wright, F. L. (1954). *The Natural House.* Horizon Press.)

Panta Rhei Heraclitus' concept that everything flows—that nothing is static, that all of existence is a current of transformation. (Cited in secondary sources, ca. 535-475 BCE)

Participatory Universe Wheeler's proposal that we live in a participatory universe—not a mechanical system, but a conscious process in which you are entangled. Consciousness is not an afterthought of matter; it is the very current shaping its flow. (Wheeler, J. A. (1994). *At Home in The Universe.* American Institute of Physics.

Phenomenology of Spirit Hegel's work exploring the development of self-consciousness and the struggle for recognition in the formation of identity. (Hegel, G. W. F. (1977). *Phenomenology Of Spirit* (A. V. Miller, Trans.). Oxford University Press. Original work published 1807)

Phoenix Effect In post-traumatic growth, reveals that people emerge from suffering with expanded compassion, deeper relationships, and clearer vision for what truly matters.

Poetics of Space Gaston Bachelard's work describing how imagination thrives in undefined spaces. It is within the unknown—the multifarious reverie—that vision takes root, creation unfolds, and the yet-to-be begins to take form. (Bachelard, G. (1994). *The Poetics of Space* (M. Jolas, Trans.). Beacon Press. Original work published 1958)

Post-Traumatic Growth Psychological phenomenon where those who suffer do not merely survive, they develop greater clarity, resilience, and purpose because of their struggles.

Principle of Accommodation and Assimilation Piaget's concept: "Every acquisition of accommodation becomes material for assimilation, but assimilation always resists new accommodations." We do not just absorb new knowledge. We reshape our very way of thinking to accommodate it. (Piaget, J. (1952). *The Origins of Intelligence In Children* (M. Cook, Trans.). International Universities Press. Original work published 1936)

Quantum Potentiality Physics concept describing energy existing in multiple states until collapsed through observation. As William James observed, your "selective interest" determines what materializes in your life.

Quantum Field Theory Scientific theory proposing that reality consists of fields extending throughout space, with particles as excitations in these fields. This supports the philosophical concept that reality is not fixed but vibrating with infinite potentials—a quantum field where all possibilities exist simultaneously, overlapping, resonating, waiting for consciousness to participate in their manifestation. (Weinberg, S. (1995). *The Quantum Theory of Fields.* Cambridge University Press.)

Reverence for Life Albert Schweitzer's profound recognition that all living beings, from the smallest blade of grass to the vast cosmos, possess an intrinsic will to exist. (Schweitzer, A. (1987). *The Philosophy of Civilization* (C. T. Campion, Trans.). Prometheus Books. Original work published 1923)

Self-Efficacy Bandura's concept that when you believe in your ability to succeed, you are more likely to take actions that align with that belief. Your sense of what's possible becomes the filter through which you perceive opportunities, shaping the path you walk and the world you encounter. (Bandura, A. (1997). *Self-Efficacy:The Exercise of Control.* W.H. Freeman and Company.)

Self-Reliance Emerson's essay with the famous quote "Trust thyself: every heart vibrates to that iron string." In that vibration, you find the resonance of your true potential. (Emerson, R. W. (1983). *Essays and Lectures.* Library of America. Original work published 1841)

Selective Interest William James' concept that what you give your attention to determines what materializes in your life. Your focused interest does not just reflect reality; it participates in creating it. This reflects his pragmatic philosophy where attention shapes experience—your conscious selection of what deserves your awareness constructs your reality. (James, W. (1890). *The Principles of Psychology.* Henry Holt and Company.)

Shadow Self Jung's concept of the hidden parts of us that surface in our interactions with others. When conflict arises, it is easy to blame the mirror—to see the other as the problem, to point outward instead of looking inward. (Jung, C. G. (1968). *The Archetypes and the Collective Unconscious* (R. F. C. Hull, Trans.). Princeton University Press. Original work published 1934)

Shoshin Zen Buddhist concept of "beginner's mind"—the ability to approach each moment as if for the first time, to see the extraordinary within the mundane, to remain open to wonder where others see routine.

System 2 Thinking Kahneman's concept of deliberate, reflective thought capable of questioning its own assumptions. (Kahneman, D. (2011). *Thinking, Fast and Slow.* Farrar, Straus and Giroux.)

Temporality Heidegger's concept that "Temporality temporalizes as a future which makes present in the process of having been." The past does not just vanish, the future does not just come to pass, the now is not a static point, they interweave. (Heidegger, M. (1962). *Being and Time* (J. Macquarrie & E. Robinson, Trans.). Harper & Row. Original work published 1927)

The One Plotinus' concept suggesting that all things emanate from a singular, infinite, and transcendent source—perfect, formless, and beyond comprehension. Through contemplation, virtue, and self-purification, the soul sheds its attachment to the lower realms and reunites with its origin. (Plotinus. (1991). *The Enneads* (S. MacKenna, Trans.). Penguin Books. Original work published ca. 270 CE)

Theory of Justice John Rawls' theory reminding us that a meaningful life is not solely measured by personal success, but by its contribution to fairness and the well-being of others. (Rawls, J. (1971). *A Theory of Justice.* Harvard University Press.)

Transcendental Idealism Kant's philosophy reminding us that we do not perceive the world as it is, but as it appears to us, filtered through our senses, cognition, and prior understanding. (Kant, I. (1998). *Critique of Pure Reason* (P. Guyer & A. W. Wood, Trans.). Cambridge University Press. Original work published 1781)

True Progress Henry David Thoreau's concept that progress is not born from passive compliance, but from the courage to resist—refusing to accept injustice or limitation as inevitable. (Thoreau, H. D. (1849*). Resistance To Civil Government.* Elizabeth Peabody.)

Uncertainty Principle Heisenberg's principle that you cannot know both the exact position and momentum of a particle. The more you define one, the more the other dissolves. So it is with your own becoming—the more rigidly you cling to "how," the more you narrow the vastness of "what could be." (Heisenberg, W. (1958). *Physics and Philosophy: The Revolution in Modern Science.* Harper & Brothers.)

Übermensch Nietzsche's concept of the one who does not settle, who transcends the self again and again, refusing stagnation. To truly live is to embrace this perpetual becoming, to reject the illusion of permanence, and to recognize that growth is not a destination but a way of being. (Nietzsche, F. (1954). *The Portable Nietzsche* (W. Kaufmann, Trans.). Viking Press. Original work published 1882)

Wabi-Sabi Japanese aesthetic centered on beauty found not in flawlessness but in the gentle wear of existence—the cracks that reveal history, the asymmetries that hold character, the unfinished edges that speak of growth still in motion.

Werden Nietzsche's concept of "becoming" as continuous transformation rather than fixed being. Identity is not a fixed state, but a continuous transformation. To truly evolve, one must embrace change, challenge self-imposed limits, and create meaning from within. (Nietzsche, F. (1954). *The Portable Nietzsche* (W. Kaufmann, Trans.). Viking Press. Original work published 1882)

Will to Believe William James' argument that belief is not a passive state but an act of will. Not about blind faith, but about the courage to commit before certainty arrives, to act despite incomplete evidence, to forge conviction through effort. (James, W. (1896). *The Will to Believe and Other Essays in Popular Philosophy*. Longmans, Green, and Co.)

Willpower Stanford psychologist Kelly McGonigal defines willpower as the ability to do what matters most, even when it is difficult—choosing long-term values over short-term urges. The warrior of will does not allow temporary pleasure to sabotage permanent greatness. (McGonigal, K. (2012). *The Willpower Instinct: How Self-Control Works, Why It Matters, and What You Can Do to Get More of It.* Avery.)

World as Will and Representation Schopenhauer's view of existence as driven by an unstoppable will, a blind force that compels all life to act. Yet humans alone possess something more: conscious will—the ability to forge action through intention, to turn instinct into mastery. (Schopenhauer, A. (1966). *The World As Will and Representation* (E. F. J. Payne, Trans.). Dover Publications. Original work published 1818)

Wu Wei Taoist concept of "non-action" or "effortless action"— accomplishing things by working with rather than against the natural flow. Like gratitude, Wu Wei is a yielding, not as resignation, but as profound trust.

Zanshin Japanese idea of relaxed alertness, the state of being fully present, yet poised to move boldly into the next moment. This equilibrium finds resonance in Taoism, where Lao Tzu wrote: "Those who flow as life flows know they need no other force."

Zeigarnik Effect Psychological principle where the brain holds onto unfinished narratives with urgency. The unknown unsettles us not because it is empty but because it is unresolved, demanding completion through our choices, our actions, our will. (Zeigarnik, B. (1927). *Über das Behalten von erledigten und unerledigten Handlungen* [On the retention of completed and uncompleted activities]. Psychologische Forschung, 9, 1-85.)

Zone of Proximal Development (ZPD) Vygotsky's concept that true growth happens not in what is comfortable, but in what is just beyond our current reach. The challenge must be enough to stretch us but not so overwhelming that we break. (Vygotsky, L. S. (1978). *Mind in Society: The Development of Higher Psychological Processes* (M. Cole, V. John-Steiner, S. Scribner, & E. Souberman, Eds.). Harvard University Press.)

ABOUT THE AUTHOR

MRIANNA is a writer and entrepreneur dedicated to inspiring ambitious minds to embrace their fullest potential.

With studies at Columbia Business School, Harvard University, and New York University, her intellectual foundation is deeply rooted in her passion for history and philosophy—disciplines she studied as an undergraduate—which continue to fuel her exploration of purpose-driven leadership and impact. She is currently an Impact Scholar, pursuing her doctorate in Organizational Change and Leadership at USC.

Alongside her fiancé, she co-leads a portfolio of ventures including a platform designed to empower the next generation of family enterprise leaders.

Inspired by the vibrancy of New York, she penned 24 LETTERS *from* NEW YORK—a collection of archetypes designed to awaken one's potential, empower self-discovery, and guide readers toward alignment with their deepest values and purpose.

To commemorate this journey, she collaborated with her grandmother to transform each letter into a one-of-a-kind painting, available at: www.iotakappa.art

MRIANNA

mrianna.com
@themrianna
contact@mrianna.com